THE RECITATION AND INTERPRETATION OF THE QUR'AN

THE RECITATION AND INTERPRETATION OF THE QUR'AN

AL-GHAZĀLĪ'S THEORY

by

MUHAMMAD ABUL QUASEM
Associate Professor
National University of Malaysia

KPI

London, Boston, Melbourne and Henley

First published in 1982
Reprinted in 1983, 1984
by KPI Limited
Routledge & Kegan Paul plc
14 Leicester Square,
London WC2H 7PH
Routledge & Kegan Paul plc
9 Park Street, Boston, Mass. 02108, USA
Routledge & Kegan Paul plc
464 St. Kilda Road, Melbourne,
Victoria 3004, Australia and
Routledge & Kegan Paul plc
Broadway House, Newtown Road,
Henley-on-Thames, Oxon RG9 1EN, England

and printed in Great Britain by
Thetford Press Limited
Thetford, Norfolk

ISBN 0-7103-0035-2

بسم الله الرحمن الرحيم

In the name of God, Most Gracious, Ever Merciful

الذين اتيناهم الكتاب يتلونه حق تلاوته. اولئك يوءمنون به؛ ومن يكفربه فاولئك
هم الخاسرون. — قرأن ١٢١ : ٢

Those whom We have given the Book (Qur'an) recite it as it should be recited; they believe in it. Those who do not believe in it are those who are the losers. — Qur'an 2 : 121

قال رسول الله صلى الله عليه وسلم: من فسر القرأن برائه فليتبوء مقعده من النار.

Whoever explains the Qur'an according to his [wrong] personal opinion shall take his place in Hell. — prophet Muḥammad

CONTENTS

INTRODUCTION

وامرت ان اكون من المسلمين، وان اتلوا القرأن. فمن اهتدى فانما يهتدى
لنفسه' ومن ضل فقل: انما انا من المنذرين. - قرأن ٩٢ - ٩١ : ٢٧

[Proclaom:] I am commanded [by God] to be one of the Muslims, and to recite the Qur'an. So whoever guides himself thereby, does so only to the good of his own self; and whoever goes astray, [does so only to his own loss]. Say: I am but a warner. — Qur'an 27 : 91 – 92

The idea underlying all revealed religions is that man is incapable of solving all the problems of his life through his reason (*'aql*) alone and therefore needs guidance from God on both the theoretical and practical levels. This guidance is embodied in religious scriptures revealed by God to prophets, who are His representatives on earth, and who are gifted with special qualities of both mind and heart. The number of such prophets whom God selected in order to communicate His guidance to mankind in different ages is generally believed by Muslims to be 124,000, and the number of revealed scriptures, according to Islamic teachings, is 104, of which four are long and of great importance, while the remaining revelations are referred to in Islamic literature only as Leaves (*ṣuḥuf*).[1] The four great scriptures are the Torah, the Gospel, the Psalms and the Qur'an, and of the Leaves ten were revealed to Adam, fifty to Shīth (Seth), thirty to Idrīs (Enoch) and ten to Abraham.[2] The Qur'an is the last in the series of these revelations, and Muḥammad (may peace be upon him!) is the last of all prophets[3] but the greatest of them in merit according to the estimation of God.[4] Muḥammad received the Qur'an gradually, over approximately twenty-three

[1] Qur'an 20:133, 87:18-19; Abū Ḥāmid Muḥammad al-Ghazālī, *Iḥyā' 'Ulūm ad-Dīn*, Beirut, n.d., III, 204.

[2] Abū Ja'far Muḥammad Ibn Jarīr aṭ-Ṭabarī, *Tārīkh al-Umam wa l-Mulūk*, Egypt, n.d., I, 86.

[3] Qur'an 33:40.

[4] Qur'an 2:235 where excellence of some prophets over others is explicit.

years (610-32 A.D.) in Mecca and Medina, from the angel of revelation, Gabriel. Gabriel had received it from the Preserved Tablet (*al-lawḥ al-maḥfūẓ*) which is commonly understood to be in heaven and where the originals of all revealed scriptures are preserved[5] along with a record of everything that God has decreed to bring into being from the beginning of creation to Doomsday,[6] under the care of the greatest angel, Isrāfīl. The Qur'an is the speech of God eternally existing with His essence; it is divine in both its meanings and language — views held by the majority of Muslims.

The reading or recitation of the Qur'an is enjoined by God and His Messenger so that the reciter may know the principles of guidance contained in it and live his life in all its aspects according to these principles; the consequence of all this is salvation (*najāt*) in the eternal life of the Hereafter. Since this purpose of Qur'an-recitation is in keeping with the sole aim of all revelations from God, it is emphasized[7] in the Qur'an as well as in prophetic tradition (*ḥadīth*). There are other purposes of Qur'an-reading which, though comparatively less important, are practically inseparable from the life of Muslims. One of these purposes is to gain the blessing (*baraka*) which accrues from uttering the divine speech with due reverence and in a proper manner. This purpose is apparent in recitations performed by Muslims at the start of sermons, in marriage ceremonies, in pious gatherings and on other occasions of a similar type. This forms a point of disagreement between Islam and Christianity. There is no absolutely holy language in the Christian religion, for the language of the Gospel is not generally believed to be wholly divine; hence Christians do not recite the Gospel to gain any blessings, nor do they respect it in the way Muslims do the Qur'an, such as keeping it above all other books on a shelf or on a table, for its language, like its meanings, is purely divine. Another purpose of Qur'an-reading is the worship (*'ibāda*) of God. Recitation for this purpose is usually performed in the morning after the Dawn Prayer, when keeping vigil at night, and on completion of every ritual prayer (*ṣalā*). It is recommended in the Qur'an and prophetic tradition as a form of supererogatory (*nafl*) worship[8] appropriate to the higher category of believers.[9] It also forms part of the spiritual training (*riyāḍa*) prescribed in ṣūfism, and is regarded

[5] Qur'an 13:39, 85:21.
[6] Qur'an 22:52; al-Ghazālī, *Iḥyā'*, IV, 504f.
[7] Qur'an 54:22, 27:92.
[8] Qur'an 17:78.
[9] See *infra*, nn. 37, 44.

in certain circumstances to be the best of all forms of supererogatory worship and in others to be only inferior to the ṣūfī's remembrance of God (*dhikr*).[10] Not only reading, but even looking at the Qur'an by a believer with due respect is also an act of worship of God.[11] Such is the glorious Qur'an, the scripture of Islam!

These and other purposes of Qur'an-reading can be better achieved if the recitation is made by following the methods appropriate to divine speech. The methodology of reading or studying books which is taught, especially in colleges and universities of the West, is not wholly relevant to the reading of the Qur'an by a believer, since its nature is different from that of other books. Some of the methods befitting it are briefly mentioned in the Qur'an itself[12] — briefly because brevity and conciseness are among its special characteristics.[13] They are, moreover, scattered in the Qur'an in connection with other teachings. The Prophet elaborated them to a certain extent and added to them other methods, and all these are to be found in works on collections of Tradition. Of all the groups of Muslim intellectuals who have flourished from the formative period of Islamic thought until now it is the ascetics and ṣūfīs who are most concerned with Qur'an-reading, because they are the people who most ardently desire to draw guidance from the Qur'an in different aspects of their lives and to improve their relationships with God by means of supererogatory worship. The rules they follow in Qur'an-reading are derived from a variety of sources, the most important of which are the Qur'an, the Sunna of the Prophet and their own experiences. Consequently a somewhat elaborate treatment of the subject of Qur'an-recitation is to be found in their mystical writings;[14] however, theological views on certain Qur'anic problems held by Jahmites, Lafẓiyyas, Wāqifiyyas, Khārijites, Murji'ites, Mu'tazilites, Ash'arites, Shī'ites and other Muslim sects are either wholly omitted in their mystical works or only mentioned in passing because these views have little relevance with practice. The orthodox form of ṣūfism of the medieval times

[10] Abū Ḥāmid Muḥammad al-Ghazālī, *al-Arba'īn fī Uṣūl ad-Dīn*, Egypt, 1344 A.H., p. 58.

[11] Al-Ghazālī, *Iḥyā'*, I, 279. [12] Qur'an 73:4, 16:98, 47:24, 4:82, 8:2, 2:121, 19:58.

[13] Abū Ḥāmid Muḥammad al-Ghazālī, *al-Qusṭās al-Mustaqīm*, ed. by al-Yasū'ī, Beirut, 1959, p. 49.

[14] Abū Ṭālib al-Makkī, *Qūt al-Qulūb*, Egypt, 1961/1381, I, 95-128 where four chapters are devoted to Qur'an-reading.

culminated in al-Ghazālī who is acclaimed by many, both in the East and the West, as the greatest religious authority of Islam after the Prophet. In his ṣūfism the problem of Qur'an-reading received a treatment [15] which is most elaborate, systematic, deep and penetrating, and which is recognized as important by later Muslim scholars of the Qur'an and Tradition. [16] This treatment is an amalgam of Islamic religious teachings on the subject and the thoughts and experiences of ṣūfīs, including al-Ghazālī himself, and other religious scholars who flourished before his time. This book is an attempt to present this theory to readers of English together with other information relevant to it.

In his theory of Qur'an-reading al-Ghazālī first mentions the nature and value of the Qur'an as well as the importance of continuance in its recitation and perseverance in its study by observing the external rules and mental tasks appropriate to it. Then he demonstrates the excellence of the Qur'an and of those who are concerned with it through reading, studying or memorizing it, by citing first the sayings of the Prophet and then the sayings of his companions and prominent scholars, saints and ṣūfīs who flourished before the time of al-Ghazālī. As a corollary of this he disapproves of those recitations which fall short of the required standard, his disapproval being based on the sayings of the Prophet, his companions and other pious scholars. This is followed by a detailed discussion of the rules of Qur'an-recitation proper. Two sets of rules are discussed under the titles 'external rules' and 'mental tasks' together with a full illustration of them in a very systematic way — passing from the external rules to the internal, and, within each set, progressing gradually from less subtle rules to more subtle. For perfect recitation both sets of rules need to be observed in al-Ghazālī's opinion. His belief that both external and internal rules are important is in agreement with Islamic religious teachings on the subject; however, his emphasis upon the mental tasks is characteristic of his ṣūfī teaching. Many of the rules set forth by him are incorporated in the work of a later scholar, Imām Muḥyī ad-Dīn an-Nawawī. [17]

Discussion of the mental tasks required in Qur'an-reading led al-Ghazālī to a consideration of the problem of Qur'an-interpreta-

[15] Al-Ghazālī, *Iḥyā'*, I, 272-93.

[16] Muḥyī ad-Dīn an-Nawawī, *al-Adhkār*, Egypt, 1378 A.H., p. 48.

[17] *Ibid.*, pp. 48-52

tion according to one's personal opinion (*bi-r-ra'y*), although this problem is not his primary concern here. This consideration proceeded through several stages. First, he establishes his view that there is a wide scope in the meanings of the Qur'an and that outward exegesis which has come down by tradition is not the end of Qur'an-understanding. In the Qur'an there are indications of all forms of knowledge which can only be grasped by men of understanding; these, however, cannot be conveyed completely by its outward exegesis. Understanding the Qur'an consists in deeply penetrating into its meanings by stages; mere outward exegesis of it does not lead us to this understanding.

Second, al-Ghazālī considers the prohibition of Qur'an-explanation according to one's personal opinion by the Prophet,[18] by Abū Bakr and by other pious Muslims in the early period of Islam. In four ways he demonstrates that this prohibition is not meant to confine Qur'an-understanding to that which has come down from authorities on exegesis and to abandon the eliciting of meanings from the Qur'an by independent understanding. He shows that it is lawful for everyone to elicit meanings from the Qur'an commensurate with his understanding and intelligence. Third, al-Ghazālī enquires into the reasons why the Prophet and others prohibited Qur'an-explanation according to one's personal opinion. Two major reasons are determined and discussed in detail. Under one of them are condemned as wrong three kinds of Qur'an-interpretation — one by heretics, one by certain religious scholars and Shī'a Bāṭinites, and one by others. In connection with the other reason he emphasizes the need to master outward exegesis of the Qur'an transmitted from authorities, as a precondition for eliciting its deep, hidden meanings. For mastering outward exegesis it is necessary to know by heart what is transmitted from authorities in regard to several Qur'anic subjects which are discussed in some detail with examples from the Qur'an itself. Then the distinction between the real meanings of the Qur'an and its outward exegesis is made clear by examples, and it is asserted that the study of the real meaning of every Qur'anic sentence needs a long duration and is assisted by knowledge obtained through mystical intuition (*kashf*). The reasons why those established in knowledge differ in their understanding of the hidden meanings of the Qur'an are mentioned. The unveiling of

[18] At-Tirmidhī, *Sunan*, Tafsīr al-Qur'an, 1.

the deep meaning of a prophetic tradition to the mind of a ṣūfī is cited, apparently following Abū Naṣr as-Sarrāj,[19] in an effort to illustrate further the nature of deep meanings of the Qur'an. In conclusion the relation of secret meanings of the Qur'an to its outward exegesis is described by saying that they are neither known by outward exegesis, nor opposed to it; rather they complete it and form the essence of the Qur'an to be approached from its external aspect.

This theory of Qur'an-recitation and interpretation outlined above is set forth in the eighth 'book' of al-Ghazālī's greatest work, *The Revival of the Religious Sciences* (*Iḥyā' 'Ulūm ad-Dīn*). This 'book' in its entirety is translated, with copious notes, in the present work, so that the reader may know al-Ghazālī's ideas in full. The translator has in his renderings, made an effort to remain very close to the Arabic original and at the same time to clarify its meaning. For the sake of this clarification materials are sometimes added in the text and put between square brackets. To ensure an easy reading some expressions based on the original are put between round brackets. To augment the usefulness of the book as well as its scholarly nature numerous footnotes are added by the translator. Since *The Revival* has not yet been critically edited, variants in its different printed texts have not yet been brought to light. The translator has at hand eight printed texts: (1) the text published by al-Maktaba at-Tijāriyya al-Kubrā, Egypt, n.d.; (2) the text published by al-Maṭba'a al-'Uthmāniyya, Egypt, 1933/1352; (3) the text published by Dār ash-Shu'ab, Egypt, n.d.; (4) the text published by the Lajna Nashr ath-Thaqāfa al-Islāmiyya, Cairo, 1356-57 A.H. (referred to hereinafter as LN): (5) the text published by Mu'assisa al-Ḥalabī, Cairo, 1967/1387 (referred to hereinafter as MH); (6) the text published by Dār al-Ma'rifa, Beirut, n.d. (referred to hereinafter as BE); (7) the text shown by az-Zabīdī in his *Itḥāf as-Sāda al-Muttaqīn bi-Sharḥ Asrār Iḥyā' 'Ulūm ad-Dīn*, Cairo, 1311 A.H. (referred to hereinafter as ZT); and (8) the text published on the margin of az-Zabīdī's *Itḥāf* (referred to hereinafter as ZE). These last mentioned five texts have been compared by the translator and the variants are pointed out in footnotes; the obvious misprints are of course disregarded. The numberings of all re-

[19] Abū Naṣr as-Sarrāj, *Kitāb al-Luma'*, ed. by R.A. Nicholson, London, 1963, p. 113.

ferences to *The Revival* in this book are as in the BE. Qur'anic verses and suras (chapters) are numbered according to the official Egyptian edition of the Qur'an. It is hoped that the book will prove useful to readers of English interested in the recitation and interpretation of Islamic scripture and in al-Ghazālī. I take this opportunity to express my gratitude to Mr. Syed Zulfida, Mr. Peter Mooney and Mr. Harold Crouch of the National University of Malaysia for carefully going through the manuscript and for reading the proofs.

National University of Malaysia
Bangi, Selangor
Muḥarram 1399
December 1978

M. Abul Quasem

TRANSLITERATION

Consonants

ء	ʼ (except when initial)	ز	z	ق	q
ب	b	س	s	ك	k
ت	t	ش	sh	ل	l
ث	th	ص	ṣ	م	m
ج	j	ض	ḍ	ن	n
ح	ḥ	ط	ṭ	ه	h
خ	kh	ظ	ẓ	و	w
د	d	ع	ʻ	ي	y
ذ	dh	غ	gh		
ر	r	ف	f		

Short Vowels

ـَ : a   ـُ : u   ـِ : i

Long Vowels

ـَى or ـَا : ā   ـُو : ū   ـِي : ī

Dipthongs

ـَيْ : ay   ـَوْ : aw   ـُوّ : uww   ـِيّ : iyy

The letter ة is sometimes transliterated into 't' and sometimes omitted.

THE RECITATION AND INTERPRETATION OF THE QUR'AN

CHAPTER ONE

THE EXCELLENCE OF THE QUR'AN AND OF PEOPLE CONCERNED WITH IT, AND THE REPROACH OF THOSE WHOSE RECITATION FALLS SHORT OF THE REQUIRED STANDARD

ان الذين يتلون كتاب الله واقاموا الصلاة وانفقوا مما رزقناهم سرا وعلانية يرجون تجارة لن تبور, ليوفيهم اجورهم ويزيدهم من فضله. — قرآن ٣٤ : ٢٩ – ٣٠

Those who recite the Book of God, observe ritual prayer, and spend out of that which We have provided for them, secretly and openly, are pursuing a commerce that suffers no loss, for God will give them their full rewards and will add to them out of His bounty. — Qur'an 34 : 29 - 30

خيركم من تعلم القرأن وعلمه

The best of you is one who has learnt the Qur'an and has taught it. — prophet Muḥammad

[PREAMBLE]

In the name of God, Most Gracious, Ever Merciful

Praise be to God Who has bestowed favour upon mankind by sending His Prophet [1] (may God bless him and greet him!) [2] and by

[1] In Islamic contexts *the* Prophet or *the* Messenger means Muḥammad, the prophet of Islam. Even when these expressions are used in a general way, not in Islamic contexts, they can legitimately mean the prophet of Islam, because he is the prototype and perfect embodiment of prophecy—prophecy started with Adam, continued through many other prophets, and reached its perfection in Muḥammad. Cf. Seyyed Hossein Nasr, *The Ideals and Realities of Islam*, 2nd ed. London, 1971, pp. 67-68 where the same view is expressed.

[2] Islam teaches that the mention of the name of any true prophet should, as a courtesy, be followed by the invoking of blessings, greetings or peace. This is especially recommended in the case of the prophet Muḥammad. There is a Qur'anic verse (33:56): "Surely God and His angels send blessings upon the Prophet. O you who believe, invoke blessings on him and salute him with the salutation of peace." In many Traditions a great reward is promised for invoking blessings, peace, salutation, and so on upon the Prophet. These Traditions are cited in al-Ghazālī's *Iḥyā'*, I,

revealing His Book [i.e. the Qur'an] 'to which falsehood cannot approach from before it or from behind it,[3] and which is a revelation from the All-wise, the All-laudable' (الذى لايأتيه الباطل من بين يديه ولا من خلفه، تنزيل من حكيم حميد)![4] In consequence of this the path of consideration from stories and reports [of past events] described in it has become broad for men of reflection,[5] and the traversing of the straight path[6] by following the rules of conduct He has expounded in it and by observing the distinction He has made between[7] the lawful and the unlawful, has become clear [to mankind].

The Qur'an is an illumination and a light; by it is obtained deliverance from error and deception; and in it lies the healing of those [diseases] which exist in men's souls.[8] Anyone, of [even] the most powerful men, who contradicts it is severely punished by God, and anyone who seeks knowledge from a source other than it is led astray by Him. The Qur'an is the strong rope of God [which man should grasp firmly], His clear light [in which man should walk in life], the strongest and most dependable support [which man should take hold of],[9] and the most perfect shelter [to which man should have recourse].

The Qur'an encompasses [the core principles of all matters —] little and much, small and great.[10] .Its wonders do not exhaust [despite the passing of ages, nor do its rare, strange features come to an end [even after deep and thorough researches]. No definition can encompass its benefits in the estimation of men of reflection, nor can much-repeated recitation make it old for those who recite it; [rather, the more-repeated its recitation the newer is it felt by them].

309-11. Some set formulae of invoking blessings upon the Prophet are long, while others are short. A few of the latter are: 'may God bless and greet him!' (صلى الله عليه وسلم), 'may God's blessing and peace be upon him!' (صلواة الله عليه وسلامه) , 'may peace be upon him!' (عليه السلام) , and 'may blessing be upon him!' (عليه الصلواة) ! Also see *infra*, nn. 14, 51.

3 This means that the Qur'an is protected from the approach of falsehood from any side. See az-Zabīdī, *op. cit.*, IV, 461.

4 Qur'an 41:42.

5 Cf. Qur'an 3:13, 12:111.

6 The straight path means the path of the truth (*ṭarīq al-ḥaqq*), i.e. the religion of Islam. See Abū l-Qāsim, Jār Allāh az-Zamakhsharī, *al-Kashshāf 'an Ḥaqā'iq at-Tanzīl*, Egypt, 1385/1966, I, 68.

7 فرق بين (ZE: فرق به بين).

8 Cf. Qur'an 17:82 — "We progressively reveal of the Qur'an that which is a [spiritual] healing and a mercy for the believers."

9 Cf. Qur'an 2:256.

10 Cf. Qur'an 6:59.

It is the Qur'an which has guided the ancients and the moderns [of Muslims] to the right path. [Even] the jinn,[11] whenever they heard its [recitation by the Prophet],[12] returned to their community with the warning, "Saying: We have certainly heard [the recitation of] a wonderful Qur'an which guides to the right path; so we have believed in it and we shall never associate anyone with our Lord" (فقالوا انا سمعنا قرانا عجبا يهدى الى الرشد، فامنابه ولن نشرك بربنا أحدا).[13] Everyone who has believed in it has indeed been favoured [by God]; one who has professed the doctrines of it has surely spoken the truth; one who has held fast to it has really become rightly guided; and one who has acted in accordance with it has certainly achieved success.

God (exalted is He!)[14] said, "Surely We Ourselves have sent down the Exhortation [i.e. the Qur'an] and We will most certainly safeguard it" (انا نحن نزلنا الذكر وانا له لحافظون).[15] Among the means of preservation of the Qur'an in men's minds and in *muṣḥafs*[16] are

[11] Jinn constitute a class of intelligent beings created by God. They are bodies (*ajsām*) composed of vapour or flames, intelligent, imperceptible to our senses, capable of appearing in different forms and of carrying out heavy labours. They are created of smokeless flame (Qur'an 55:15). They are capable of salvation; they fall under religious obligation (Qur'an 51:56, 55:39, 60:128, 6:130); some jinn will enter Paradise while others will be cast into Hell (Qur'an 7:38, 179). They can mix with men. There are stories of love between jinn and human beings. There are many stories too of relations between saints and jinn; see Ibn an-Nadīm, *Kitāb al-Fihrist*, trans. by Bayard Dodge, New York, 1970, pp. 209, 291, 539, 728-29, 756-57, 760 823; D.B. Macdonald, H. Masse *et al*, "Djinn", *EI*², II, 546-50.

[12] Two years before his migration (*hijra*) to Medina the Prophet went to Ta'if to preach Islam and to seek a protector in view of the increasingly humiliating treatment to which he was subjected after the death of his uncle, Abū Ṭālib. On his way back to Mecca when he was engaged in supererogatory ritual prayer at midnight at Nakhla a company of jinn came, listened and went off believing him and the Qur'an. See *Ibn* Hishām, *as-Sīra an-Nabawiyya*, ed. by Muṣṭafā as-Saqā *et al*, 2nd ed., Egypt, 1955/1375, I, 421f.; Qur'an 72:1, 46:29.

[13] Qur'an 72:1.

[14] Islam teaches that the mention of the divine name should be followed by such formulae of praise as: 'exalted is He!' (تعالى), 'great and mighty is He!' (عزوجل), 'glorified (or holy) is He!' (سبحانه), 'great and exalted is He!' (جل وعلى), and 'blessed and exalted is He!' (تبارك وتعالى). This is the requirement of courtesy (*adab*) in respect of the divine name.

[15] Qur'an 15:9.

[16] A *muṣḥaf* is a book or volume consisting of a collection of leaves written upon and put between two covers. It is generally applied in the present day to a copy of the Qur'ān. For more information on it see A.J. Wensinck, "Muṣḥaf", *EI*, III, 747; Edward William Lane, *An Arabic-English Lexicon*, ed. by Stanley Lane-Poole, London, Bk. I, Pt. 4, p. 1655.

continuance in its recitation and perseverance in its study, by following its rules (*ādāb*)[17] and stipulations and by carefully observing the mental tasks and the external rules which concern it.[18] These matters need to be discussed and expounded, and what is intended to teach here can be made very clear in four chapters:

The first chapter deals with the excellence of the Qur'an and of people concerned with it (*ahlihi*). The second chapter is on the rules of the Qur'an-recitation to be observed externally. The third chapter concerns the mental tasks (*al-a'māl al-bāṭina*) to be performed when the Qur'an is recited. The fourth chapter discusses the understanding of the Qur'an, its exegesis by personal opinion (*bi r-ra'y*),[19] and so on.

THE EXCELLENCE OF THE QUR'AN

[Prophetic Traditions on the Excellence of the Qur'an]

The Prophet (may God bless him and greet him!) said, "A man who reads the Qur'an and who then feels that another man has been bestowed [by God] more than what he himself has been bestowed, has indeed considered small that which God (exalted is He!) has considered great." [272]

The Prophet (may God bless him and greet him!) said, "In the Hereafter no intercessor will be superior in rank in the estimation of God (exalted is He!) to the Qur'an — not [even] a prophet, nor an angel, nor anyone else."[20]

[17] *Adab* (plural: *ādāb*) in this context means a rule to be followed. In this sense it occurs many times in the first part of al-Ghazālī's *Iḥyā'*. For its meanings in various other contexts see Lane, *Lexicon*, Bk. I, Pt. I, 34-35; F. Gabrieli, "Adab", *EI*², I, 175-176.

[18] Observance of both the external rules and mental tasks of Qur'an-reading is necessary because without it the purpose of Qur'an-reading cannot be achieved fully. Al-Ghazālī's consideration of the internal aspect of Qur'an-recitation as important, in addition to its external aspect, is mystical in nature. Not only in Qur'an-reading but in all other forms of Islamic devotional acts, he lays importance upon both aspects. For a brief account of this see Muhammad Abul Quasem, *The Ethics of al-Ghazālī*, 2nd ed., New York, 1978, pp. 194-207.

[19] This refers to a Tradition (at-Tirmidhī, *Sunan*, Tafsīr al-Qur'an, 1) which runs thus: "The man who explains the Qur'an according to his personal opinion shall take his place in Hell."

[20] In the Hereafter angels, prophets, saints, martyrs, pious religious scholars, and the Qur'an will intercede to God on behalf of believers. They, however, will be able to

The Prophet (may God bless him and greet him!) said, "If the Qur'an were inside a hide, fire could not touch the hide because of the blessings of its contact with the Qur'an." [21]

The Prophet (may God bless him and greet him!) said, "[One of] the best devotional acts (*'ibādāt*) of my community is the recitation of the Qur'an."

The Prophet (may God bless him and greet him!) also said, "God (great and mighty is He!) had read the Sura of Ṭā Hā [22] and the Sura of Yā Sīn [23] a thousand years before He created the creation. When angels heard the Qur'an they said, 'Blessed is the community to which it will be sent down, blessed are the minds which will bear it, and blessed are the tongues which will utter it."

The Prophet (may God bless him and greet him!) said, "The best of you is one who has learnt the Qur'an and has taught it," [24]

intercede only with God's permission (Qur'an 2:255, 21:28, 10:3, 19:87, 20:109, 34:23, 53:26). This intercession will be in some cases for elevation of rank in Paradise, in some for admission into Paradise without suffering in Hell, and in most cases to rescue the sinful believers from Hell after suffering there for sometime. The prophet Muḥammad will be granted permission to intercede for Muslims (al-Bukhārī, *Sahīh*, Da'wāt, 1, 'Ilm, 33, Riqāq, 51, Anbiyā', 9; Muslim, *Ṣaḥīḥ*, Īmān, 302, 318, 326, 334-45, Zuhd, 38; Abū Dāwūd, *Sunan*, 21; Ibn Ḥanbal, *Musnad*, IV, 434; Ibn Māja, *Sunan*, Zuhd, 37). Every Muslim should pray to God that He may grant the Prophet permission to intercede for him. Concerning the intercession of the Qur'an, there is a 'sound' Tradition in Muslim's *Ṣaḥīḥ*, Musāfirīn, 252: The Prophet said, "Read the Qur'an, for it will come, on the Day of Resurrection, as an intercessor for its reader."

[21] The meaning is that the untanned, dry hide is destroyed and burnt by fire much more quickly and easily than the tanned hide. A negligible thing, it is not taken much care of and is sometimes thrown into fire. The Qur'an is so great that even if it is kept inside this negligible and easily destroyable thing it will not burn because of the blessings of its contact with the Qur'an. How, then, is it possible that the fire of Hell should burn a believer who memorizes the glorious Qur'an and perseveres in its memorization, and keeps all his duties towards it? Hell-fire cannot burn him.

[22] This is the twentieth sura of the Qur'an consisting of one hundred and thirty-five verses. It was revealed before the *hijra*, the Prophet's migration to Medina.

[23] This is the thirty-sixth Qur'anic sura consisting of eighty-three verses. The Prophet called it "the heart of the Qur'an"(قلب القرآن). See Aḥmad Ibn Ḥanbal, *Musnad*, V, 26. It is greatly admired by Muslims and is frequently recited: Pious Muslims recite it after every ritual prayer (*ṣalā*), at keeping vigil at night (*qiyām al-layl*), and when visiting the grave of a Muslim. There is a Tradition to the effect that if a person, on entering into the graveyard, recites this sura and offers its reward to the dead, God lightens the punishment of those buried in it for that day, and he obtains the reward of acts equal to the number of them.

[24] Al-Bukhārī, *Ṣaḥīḥ*, Faḍā'il al-Qur'an, 21; Ibn Māja, *Sunan*, Muqaddama, 16;

The Prophet (may God bless him and greet him!) said, "God (blessed and exalted is He!) says, 'The man whom Qur'an-reading has prevented from supplicating to Me and making petition to Me, is given by Me the best of the reward of those who are grateful [to Me].'"[25]

The Prophet (may God bless him and greet him!) said, "On the Day of Resurrection three men will be on the heap of black [i.e. the best quality] musk. No dread will overtake them, and no reckoning find them until that with which the people will be occupied is over. One of these three men is he who reads the Qur'an seeking the face of God (great and mightly is He!). Another is he who leads a group of people in ritual prayer in a way that pleases them."[26]

The Prophet (may God bless him and greet him!) said, "Those who are concerned with the Qur'an (*ahl al-Qur'an*) are friends of God and are special to Him."[27]

The Prophet (may God bless him and greet him!) said, "Human souls become rusty just as iron becomes rusty." On being asked, "Messenger of God, how can they be polished?", he replied, "Through recitation of the Qur'an and remembrance of death."

The Prophet (may God bless him and greet him!) said, "God certainly listens to a Qur'an-reader much more than does the owner of a songstress to her."[28]

Sayings of the Prophet's Companions and Other Pious Muslims in Early Islam [on the Excellence of the Qur'an]

Abū Umāma al-Bāhilī[29] said, "Read the Qur'an and let not these

ad-Dārimī, *Sunan*, Faḍā'l al-Qur'an, 2.

[25] At-Tirmidhī, *Sunan,* Thawāb al-Qur'an, 25; ad-Dārimī, *Sunan*, Faḍā'il al-Qur'an, 6.

[26] The third man not mentioned here is one who summons people to ritual prayer five times every day and night. See at-Tirmidhī, *Sunan*, birr, 54, Janna, 25 (in an abridged form); Ibn Ḥanbal, *Musnad*, II, 26.)

[27] Ibn Ḥanbal, *Musnad*, III, 128, 242. 'Those who are concerned with the Qur'an' means those believers who safeguard it and cleave to it by reciting and memorizing it and by acting in accordance with its teachings. See az-Zabīdī, *op. cit.*, IV, 465.

[28] Ibn Māja, *Sunan*, Iqāma, 176; Ibn Ḥanbhal, *Musnad*, VI, 19, 20.

[29] Abū Umāma al-Bāhilī (d. 81 or 86 A.H.) was a companion of the Prophet and a prolific narrator of Tradition. According to some authorities, he was the last of those

suspended *muṣḥafs* deceive you at all, for God will not punish a soul which has contained the Qur'an [by memorizing it, pondering over it and acting in accordance with it]."

Ibn Mas'ūd[30] said, "When you intend to acquire knowledge, deeply study the Qur'an for in it lies the [principles of] knowledge of the ancients and the moderns (*'ilm al-awwalīn wa l-ākharīn*)." [31]

He also said, "Read the Qur'an, for you will be rewarded at the rate of [the recompense of] ten good deeds for reading every letter of the Qur'an. Take notice, I do not say that *alif lām mīm* (الم)[32] constitute one letter. Rather [I should say that] *alif* (ا) is one letter, *lām* (ل) is another, and *mīm* (م) is [still] another."

He further said, "None of you will ask about himself to anyone except the Qur'an: If he loves it and admires it [this is a sign that] he loves God (glorified is He!) and His Messenger (may God bless him and greet him!). If, however, he hates the Qur'an [this is a proof that] he hates God (glorified is He!) and His Messenger (may God bless him and greet him!)." [33]

companions of the Prophet who died in Syria. For his biography see Ibn Ḥajar al-'Asqalānī, *al-Iṣāba*, Egypt, 1358/1939, IV, 10; Ibn 'Abd al-Barr, *al-Istī'āb*, in Ibn Ḥajar, *op. cit.*, IV, 4f.

30 'Abd Allāh Ibn Mas'ūd (d. 32 A.H./652-53 A.D.), a famous companion of the Prophet, was a very early convert to Islam — either the third or the sixth in order. He embraced Islam immediately after seeing a miracle of the Prophet: The Prophet touched the udders of a barren ewe which gave no milk, and she then gave milk. He used to carry the Prophet's sandals and to gather the wood from which the Prophet's tooth-stick were made. Thus he was daily in close contact with the Prophet. He took part in many battles including those of Badr (2 A.H.), Uḥud (3 A.H.), and the Yarmūk (13 A.H.). After the Prophet's death he also acted as an administrator, an ambassador, and a missionary. A great narrator of Traditions, an authority on Qur'an-reading, Qur'anic exegesis, and legal matters, he was one of those Companions who were held in high esteem for their shrewdness, learning and integrity. See Ibn 'Abd al-Barr, *op. cit.*, II, 308-16; Ibn Ḥajar, *op. cit.*, II, 360ff.; Ibn Qutayba, *al-Ma'ārif*, ed. by Tharwat 'Ukāsha, Cairo, 1969, pp. 249-51.

31 Al-Ghazālī attributes much value to this saying of Ibn Mas'ūd; he repeatedly quotes it in his books. See *infra*, p. 88; *al*-Ghazāli, *Jawāhir al-Qur'an*, 2nd ed., Cairo, 1933, p. 8. Other ṣūfīs, especially al-Makkī (*Qūt*, I, 103), have also quoted this saying.

32 These are names of three Arabic letters. They occur at the start of several other suras as well. Other Arabic letters occur in the beginning of several other suras. These letters are called the *ḥurūf muqaṭṭa'āt* of the Qur'an. Various explanations have been given of their occurrence and significance: al-Ghazālī (*infra* p. 91) speaks of seven; since his time a few more explanations have been put forward.

33 Islam teaches that love of God and of His prophet Muḥammad is the highest

'Amr Ibn al-'Āṣ[34] said, "Every verse of the Qur'an is [like] a stair of Paradise and a lamp in your houses."

He also said, "A man who reads the Qur'an, thereby includes prophethood between the two sides of his body. However, no revelation will be revealed to him."

Abū Hurayra[35] said [273], "Surely the house in which the Qur'an is recited provides easy circumstances for its people, its good increases, angels come to it [in order to listen to the Qur'an] and Satans leave it. The house in which the Book of God (great and mighty is He!) is not recited provides difficult circumstances for its people, its good decreases, angels leave it and Satans come to it."

Aḥmad Ibn Ḥanbal[36] said, "I saw God (great and mighty is He!) in my dream and asked Him, 'Lord how have those who have drawn

ideal of man (Qur'an 9:24). The stronger is this love the happier will he be in the Hereafter. One who loves God and the Prophet will love the Qur'an necessarily, since it is God's words transmitted to mankind by the Prophet. Islamic religious teachings on love of God, the Prophet and the Qur'an are strongly emphasized by such great ṣūfīs as al-Ghazālī, al-Makkī and al-Ḥasan al-Baṣrī. See al-Ghazālī, *Iḥyā'*, IV, 294-337; Quasem, *Ethics*, pp. 64-78, 181-93.

34 'Amr Ibn al-'Āṣ (d. 51 or 42 A.H.) was a companion of the Prophet and a very witty politician. The Prophet made use of his assistance in military expeditions and political affairs. He made a great contribution to the expansion of Islam outside Arabia during the caliphates of Abū Bakr and 'Umar. The conquest of Egypt and of the country west of the Jordan is his special achievement. He remained the governor of Egypt until his death. See Ibn Qutayba, *op. cit.*, pp. 285f.

35 Abū Hurayra (d. 58 or 59 A.H.) was a companion of the Prophet and a prolific narrator of Traditions — prolific because he stayed with the Prophet most of the time and because the Prophet prayed to God for an increase in his memory. He was one of the poor men called 'the People of Veranda' (*ahl aṣ-ṣuffa*) and is particularly respected by the ṣūfīs, including al-Ghazālī. Among those Companions who emigrated to Medina leaving their houses and belongings, there were some who were very poor (Qur'an 59:8, 2:273) and who used to lodge at the veranda of the Prophet's Mosque, devoting their entire time to religious practices. They are the embodiment of 'poverty' (*faqr*), a ṣūfīstic virtue, and are therefore highly respected by the ṣūfīs. After the Prophet's death Abū Hurayra continued to practise 'poverty' but at the same time took part in the administration. He had great reputation for piety. See Ibn Ḥajar, *op. cit.*, IV, 200-208; Ibn 'Abd al-Barr, *op. cit.*, IV, 200-207; W. Montgomery Watt, "Ahl al-Ṣuffa," *EI*², I, 266-67; al-Hujwīrī, *Kashf al-Maḥjūb*, trans, by R.A. Nicholson, Leyden, 1911, p. 19.

36 Aḥmad Ibn Ḥanbal (d. 241 A.H./855 A.D.) was a celebrated jurist and Traditionist, and the founder of the Ḥanbalī school (*madhhab*) of Islamic jurisprudence. He was one of the most vigorous personalities who profoundly influenced the historical development of Islam and its modern revival. He was a devotee, an ascetic,

near to You[37] achieved this nearness?' God replied, 'By My speech [i.e. the Qur'an], O Aḥmad.' "Aḥmad said, "I enquired, 'Lord, by understanding [the meaning of] Your speech [in which they have belief] or without understanding it?' God replied, 'By understanding as well as without understanding.' "

Muḥammad Ibn Ka'b al-Qurẓī[38] said, "When the people hear the Qur'an from God (great and mighty is He!) on the Day of Resurrection, they will feel [as if] they have never heard it before."

Al-Fuḍayl Ibn 'Iyāḍ[39] said, "A man holding the Qur'an [by committing it to memory and by acting in accordance with it], should have no need of anyone [i.e. need not debase himself before anyone in having any of his needs fulfilled] — not even of the caliphs and their political subordinates [who mostly belong to the worldings]. Rather the needs of people should be directed towards him [in reverence of the Qur'an he is holding]."

He also said, "A man bearing the Qur'an is [in effect] bearing the standard of Islam. So magnifying his duty towards the Qur'an he should not make unlawful amusement with one who makes unlawful

a learned man versed in the knowledge of the Hereafter, a jurist with complete understanding of man's well being in this life, and one who, in all his pursuits, sought only the pleasure of God. See al-Ghazālī, *Iḥyā'*, I, 24.

37 In the Qur'an human beings are classified into three broad categories, namely, the people on the left (*aṣḥāb ash-shimāl*), the people on the right (*aṣḥāb al-yamīn*), and those drawn near to God (*al-muqarrabūn*). The first consists of those who deny God and His messengers (*al-mukadhdhibūn*). They are also called those who have gone astray (*aḍ-ḍāllūn*). The second category is made up of believers. In the last category are placed those who are most pious believers. They are also called those who are foremost (*as-sābiqūn*). See Qur'an 56:7-94, 7:36-53. Corresponding to these two categories of believers two grades of virtuous acts are prescribed in the Qur'an and Tradition — the higher grade is for the most pious believers and the lower for those who are only ordinarily pious. Recitation of the Qur'an belongs to the higher grade of virtuous acts.

38 Muḥammad Ibn Ka'b al-Qurẓī (d. 108 or 117 or 118 A.H.) was a great Follower (*tābi'ī*), i.e. a Muslim who did not see the Prophet but saw his companions. He was a reliable (*thiqa*) narrator of Tradition and a famous teacher of the Qur'an. See az-Zabīdī, *op. cit.*, IV, 466; Ibn Qutayba, *op. cit.*, pp. 458f.

39 Fuḍayl Ibn 'Iyāḍ (d. 187 A.H./803 A.D.) was an ascetic and an early ṣūfī. He deeply studied Tradition and became a famous transmitter of it. Following the Qur'an (35:28) he taught that fear of God is caused by knowledge of Him. He stressed asceticism of the world and satisfaction (*riḍā'*) with the decree of God. See as-Sulamī, *Ṭabaqāt aṣ-Ṣūfiyya,* ed. by Nūr ad-Dīn, Egypt, 1953/1372, pp. 6-14; al-Hujwīrī, *Kashf,* pp. 97f.; Ibn Qutayba, *op. cit.*, p. 511.

amusement, should not be unmindful of his duties with one who is unmindful, and should not utter nonsense to one who utters nonsense. [Rather he should pardon them and forgive them]."

Sufyān ath-Thawrī[40] said, "When a man reads the Qur'an [seeking the pleasure of God], the angel [who arrives to listen to it] kisses him between his two eyes [paying respect to him and to the Qur'an he has read]."

'Amr Ibn Maymūn[41] said, "If a man, on performing the Dawn Prayer, opens the *muṣḥaf* and reads from it a hundred verses, God (great and mighty is He!) raises this good deed like the good deeds of all people of the world."[42]

It is related that Khālid Ibn 'Uqba[43] [once] came to the Messenger of God (may God bless him and greet him!) and entreated, "Read to me [some verses of] the Qur'an." The Prophet read, "Surely God enjoins justice, beneficence and giving to kinsmen, and forbids indecency, wrong conduct and transgression; He admonishes you that you may take heed" (ان الله يأمر بالعدل والاحسان وايتاء ذى القربى، وينهى عن الفحشاء والمنكر والبغى، يعظكم لعلكم تذكرون).[44] Khālid

40 Sufyān ath-Thawrī (d. 161 A.H./778 A.D.) was a celebrated jurist and Traditionist, and an ascetic of the highest order. His fame as a Traditionist spread on account of the extraordinary breadth of his knowledge and his reliability. He founded an independent school (*madhhab*) of jurisprudence which, however, did not last long. His deep piety was well known. Ṣūfīs such as al-Ghazālī and al-Makkī frequently quote his sayings. See al-Ghazālī, *Iḥyā'*, I, 24, 28; Ibn Qutayba, *op. cit.*, pp. 497f.

41 'Amr Ibn al-Maymūn, also called Ibn ar-Ramāḥ (d. 171 A.H.), was a reliable Traditionist and a devoted Qur'an-reciter. He memorized the Qur'ān in its entirety and was very conscious of his responsibilities towards it. See az-Zabīdī, *op. cit.*, IV, 467.

42 On the excellence of especially reciting a hundred verses of the Qur'an also spoke such great companions of the Prophet as Anas, Ḥudhayfa, Abū d-Dardā', and Tamīm ad-Dārī. See *ibid.*

43 See Ibn al-Athīr, *Usd al-Ghāba*, Egypt, 1280 A.H., II, 97f.; Ibn Ḥajar *op. cit.*, I, 410; Ibn 'Abd al-Barr, *op. cit.*, I, 411.

44 Qur'an 16:90. This is a very important verse of the Qur'an, and it is with this verse that the *imām* of the Friday Assembly Prayer concludes his sermon, because a perfect gradation of moral values has been prescribed in this verse. On the negative side, not only must every kind of trespass against person, property and honour be eschewed; but unmannerly behaviour and evil thoughts and desires must also be guarded against. On the positive side, there are two grades: Lower and higher. At the lower grade of value one must do justice, i.e. must return good for good and exact only proportionate retribution for a wrong suffered. But the man who is at the higher grade and who seeks the pleasure of God must be benevolent; that is, he must render good without any thought of return, and forgive wrongs and injuries till beneficence

entreated, "Repeat [the recitation of the Qur'an]." The Prophet repeated. Then Khālid said, "I swear, it is sweet and elegant, its lower part is putting forth leaves and its upper part is bearing fruits, it is not the speech of any human being."[45]

Al-Ḥasan[46] said, "I swear by God, besides the Qur'an there is no sufficiency [i.e. one who believes in the Qur'an has sufficiency the like of which is non-existent], and after [the deprivation of belief in] the Qur'an there is no poverty [more severe]."

Al-Fuḍayl[47] said, "A man who reads the end of the Sura of Gathering[48] [at night] until the morning and then dies on that very day, is stamped with the stamp of martyrs. A man who reads it in the evening and then dies in that very night, is stamped with the stamp of martyrs."

Al-Qāsim Ibn 'Abd ar-Raḥmān[49] said, "I said to a certain devotee, 'There is no one here with whom we may establish friendly relations." [Having heard this] the devotee extended his hand to the *muṣḥaf* [that was by his side] and, putting it on his chest, said, '[With] this [you should establish friendly relations].' "

'Alī Ibn Abī Ṭālib[50] (may God be pleased with him!)[51] said,

towards fellow-men becomes part of his nature and flows out of him as naturally as affection for close kindred. These two grades of values are in accordance with the two categories of the virtuous taught in the Qur'an, namely, the righteous and those drawn near to God. Also see *supra*, n. 37.

45 Ibn 'Abd al-Barr, *op. cit.*, I, 411; Ibn Ḥajar, *op. cit.*, I, 410; Ibn al-Athīr, *op. cit.*, II, 97f. (with slight variation).

46 Al-Ḥasan al-Baṣrī (d. 110 A.H./728 A.D.), a Follower, was a great ṣūfī, a real ascetic, a sincere preacher, a famous theologian, and a learned Traditionist. His sayings are often quoted in literatures on different Islamic subjects. His *Risāla* contains valuable knowledge. See Ibn Qutayba, *op. cit.*, pp. 440f.

47 See *supra*, n. 39.

48 The end of the Sura of Gathering (*ākhir al-Ḥashr*) is the last three verses of the fifty-ninth sura of the Qur'an (59:22-24). Pious Muslims recite them on completion of every ritual prayer and when keeping vigil at night. The importance of these verses lies in their reference to the unity of God, His beautiful names denoting His attributes, and His works — things which constitute the aims of the Qur'an. These verses, in al-Ghazālī's opinion, are only comparable to the Verse of the Throne (*āyat al-kursī*) (2:255), and to the beginning of the Sura of Iron (*awwal al-Ḥadīd*) (57:1-6). See Muḥammad Abul Quasem, *The Jewels of the Qur'an: al-Ghazālī's Theory*, 1977, pp. 75-78.

49 Al-Qāsim Ibn 'Abd ar-Raḥman (d. 113 A.H.), a Follower, was a Traditionist who transmitted Traditions from several companions of the Prophet. See az-Zabīdī, *op. cit.*, IV, 468.

50 'Alī Ibn Abī Ṭālib (d. 42 A.H.) was a cousin and son-in-law of the Prophet and

"There are three things which increase memory and remove phlegm.[52] They are: Cleaning the teeth with a tooth-stick, fasting, and reading the Qur'an."

THE REPROACH OF QUR'AN-RECITATION BY UNMINDFUL PEOPLE

Anas Ibn Mālik[53] said, "It often happens that a man recites the Qur'an, and the Qur'an curses him."[54]

Maysara said,[55] "The Qur'an is a stranger in the mind of a

the fourth rightly-guided caliph. He was one of the first to believe in Islam — either the second or the third in order. He embraced Islam when he was a boy of ten or eleven at most. Very strong both physically and mentally, he always displayed a high degree of courage. His service to the cause of Islam both during and after the Prophet's lifetime was tremendous. He had profound knowledge of the Qur'an and the Sunna; the other three caliphs who preceded him used to ask his advice especially on legal matters. He was one of the best readers and exegetes of the Qur'an. His gifts as an orator were remarkable. He was also endowed with poetic art. His austerity, his vigorous observance of religious rites, and his detachment from worldy goods are especially admired by the ascetics and ṣūfīs who often quote his sayings. See Ibn Qutayba, *op. cit.*, pp. 203-18; Ibn 'Abd al-Barr, *op. cit.*, III, 26-67.

51 Islamic courtesy (*adab*) requires that the mention of a name of a companion of the Prophet should be followed by the supplication, 'may God be pleased with him!' (رضي الله عنه). In the case of 'Alī Ibn Abī Ṭālib especially, one may supplicate by another formula: 'may God honour his face!'(كرم الله وجهه). Also see *supra*, nn. 2, 14.

52 These are the non-religious benefits. The religious benefits have not been mentioned here. These can be indicated by citing a few Traditions: Regarding the tooth-stick the Prophet said, "The use of a tooth-stick ... pleases the Lord" (al-Bukhārī, *Ṣaḥīḥ*, ṣawm 27; an-Nasā'ī, *Sunan*, Ṭahāra, 4). He also said, "One ritual prayer after the use of the tooth-stick is better than seventy ritual prayers without the use of it" (Ibn Ḥanbal, *Musnad*, Ṭahāra, 169). Concerning fasting the Prophet said, "God says, 'Every good act is recompensed by the reward of an act greater than it from ten to seven hundred times; fasting is an exception to this, for it is observed for Me and it is I Who shall recompense it' " (al-Bukhārī, *Ṣaḥīḥ*, Ṣawm, 2; Muslim, *Ṣaḥīḥ*, Ṣiyām, 164, 165; Ibn Māja, *Sunan*, Ṣiyām, 1). The Prophet also said, "Paradise has a gate called the Rayyān. Only those who fast will enter into Paradise through it..." (al-Bukhārī, *Ṣaḥīḥ*, Ṣawm, 9; Muslim, *Ṣaḥīḥ*, Siyām, 162, 164, 165).

53 Anas Ibn Mālik (d. 91 or 93 A.H.) was a companion of the Prophet and a prolific transmitter of Tradition. His mother gave him to the Prophet as a servant at the age of eight. He remained in the Prophet's service until the latter's death. Later on he took part in the wars of conquest. See Ibn Ḥajar, *op. cit.*, I, 84f.

54 How a Qur'an-reciter is often cursed by the Qur'an itself is explained in the saying of a religious scholar in *infra*, p. 31.

55 Maysara al-Ashja'ī was a Traditionist. He narrated Traditions from Abū Ḥāzim and Sa'īd Ibn al-Musayyib. See az-Zabīdī, *op. cit.*, IV, 468.

profligate (*fājir*)[56] [— stranger because he bears it only for ostentation (*riyā'*), and does not act in accordance with its teachings]."

Abū Sulaymān ad-Dārānī[57] said, "Guards of Hell (*az-zabāniyya*)[58] will hasten to those holders of the Qur'an who disobey God (great and mightly is He!) more than to the worshippers of idols, since they disobey God (glorified is He!) after [holding] the Qur'an."

A certain religious scholar said, "When a son of Adam [i.e. man] reads the Qur'an, then mingles [good with evil], and then turns [to God] and reads it again, he is asked [by God], 'What is your relationship with My speech?' "

Ibn ar-Ramāḥ said, "I am ashamed of knowing the Qur'an by heart, for I am told that people concerned with the Qur'an will be asked [by God] concerning that of which prophets will be asked on the Day of Resurrection."

Ibn Mas'ūd said, "The holder of the Qur'an should realize [the value of] his nightime when people are asleep, of his daytime when people commit excesses, of his grief when people are joyful, of his weeping when people laugh, of his silence when people are engaged in vain talk, and of his humility when people have a haughty deportment. The holder of the Qur'an should be gentle and soft minded; he should not be harsh, nor quarrelsome, nor one who shouts much, nor one who makes strong noises in markets, nor a man of hasty temper who gets angry quickly."

56 A Muslim is considered profligate (*fājir*) if he adheres to the faith in his mind, professes it in his words, performs certain acts prescribed by the Sharī'a, but has committed many great sins (*kabā'ir*). He is identical with *fāsiq*. In the Hereafter he can be punished in Hell in proportion to his sins, but must ultimately be sent to Paradise. The Prophet said, "Those whose minds contain only a particle of faith will leave Hell" (al-Bukhārī, *Ṣaḥīḥ*, Īmām, 33), and the profligate has faith, though it is very weak. See al-Ghazālī, *Iḥyā'*, I, 117, 119f.

57 Abū Sulaymān ad-Dārānī (d. 205 or 215 A.H.) was a noted ascetic and a ṣūfī who defined asceticism as the abandonment of everything which stands in the way between man and God. This definition is accepted by later ṣūfīs especially al-Ghazālī (Quasem, *Ethics*, p. 169). His sayings on other spiritual themes are often quoted by the ṣūfīs who came after him. See al-Hujwīrī *Kashf*, 112f.; as-Sulamī, *op. cit.*, pp. 75-82.

58 *Az-Zabāniyya* means those angels who guard Hell (Qur'an 96:18); they are extremely rough and violent (Qur'an 66:6). They are nineteen in number (Qur'an 74:30). The keeper of Hell is a different angel whose name is Mālik. See Qur'an 43:77.

The Prophet (may God bless him and greet him!) said, "Most of the ostentatious people of this community [i.e. the community of Muslims] will be its Qur'an-readers, [since they will pretend that they read the Qur'an only for pleasing God, whereas what will in fact be present in their minds is the desire for pleasing people for worldly advantages]."[59]

The Prophet (may God bless him and greet him!) said, "Read the Qur'an so long as it enables you to desist [from what is prohibited by it and to follow what is commanded by it]. If it has not enabled you to desist [from the things prohibited by it] you have not read it [i.e. not been benefited by it]."

The Prophet (may God bless him and greet him!) said, "One who considers lawful the things declared unlawful in the Qur'an does not believe in it."[60]

A certain righteous father (*ba'ḍ as-salaf*) said [274], "There is a man who starts the reading of a Qur'anic sura, and angels bless him until he completes it. There is another man who starts the reading of a Qur'anic sura, and angels curse him until he completes it." On being asked, "How is this possible?", he replied, "If the reader of the sura [practically] considers lawful the things declared lawful therein, and if he [practically] considers unlawful the things declared unlawful therein, then angels bless him. But if he does not do so, angels curse him."

A certain religious scholar said, "Surely a man recites the Qur'an, and thereby curses himself without being aware of it: He recites [the verse], 'Take notice, God's curse is on wrongdoing people!' (الا لعنة الله على الظالمين),[61] whereas he is a wrongdoer himself; he recites [the verse], 'Take notice, God's curse is on the liars!' (الا لعنة الله على الكاذبين),[62] whereas he is one of them."

Al-Ḥasan said [to Qur'an-readers], "You have adopted the recitation of the Qur'an in stages (*marāḥil*) and have made the night [as if] a camel; by riding on it you pass the stages of the Qur'an. But those before you regarded it [as consisting of] messages which came from their Lord; they used to ponder over them at night and execute them by day."[63]

[59] Aḥmad Ibn Ḥanbal, *Musnad*, II, 175, 4, 101.

[60] Al-Tirmidhī, *Sunan*, Thawāb al-Qur'an, 20.

[61] Qur'an 11:18. [62] Qur'an 3:61.

[63] From this saying of al-Ḥasan it is clear how great an emphasis the ṣūfis lay first

Idn Mas'ūd said, "The Qur'an is sent down to people in order that they may act in accordance with its teachings; but they have taken up mere study of it as a duty. Certainly one of you reads the Qur'an from its beginning to its end [so thoroughly that] not a single letter of it is dropped out of his reading, whereas to act in accordance with it is dropped out."

In the Tradition of Ibn 'Umar[64] and the Tradition of Jundab[65] (may God be pleased with them both!) [it is mentioned that they said]: "We have lived for a long time and [have seen that] one of us was granted the faith (*īmān*) [by God] prior to [the revelation of certain suras of] the Qur'an; then he, when a sura was revealed to Muḥammad (may God bless him and greet him!), learned about lawful and unlawful, commandments and threats set forth in that sura, and [also] those places of it where he should pause (*waqf*). Then, a time came when I saw a man who was given the Qur'an prior to his acceptance of the faith; he read all the pages between the Opening Sura of the Book and its end, without realizing what are its commandments, what are its threats, and which are those places of it where he should pause — he scattered it like the scattering of one flying away."

It has occurred in the Torah: "Man, are you not ashamed of Me? [Sometimes] a letter comes to you from a certain friend while you are walking along the road; turning aside from the road you sit, read the letter and ponder over each word of it so that no part of it is missed.

on understanding the meanings of the Qur'an and then on acting in accordance with what they understand of these meanings. The ṣūfīs are men of action, not of mere theories.

64 'Abd Allāh Ibn 'Umar (d. 73 A.H./693 A.D.) was one of the most prominent companions of the Prophet who are most frequently quoted for Traditions. He was greatly admired by his contemporaries for his high moral qualities and deep piety. In transmitting Traditions he was most scrupulous in neither adding to nor omitting anything from the Traditions narrated by him. He took part in many expeditions during and after the Prophet's lifetime, but, keeping himself mostly away from administration, he devoted all his time to religious practices. See Ibn Ḥajar, *op. cit.*, II, 338-41.

65 Abū Dharr Jundab al-Ghifārī (d. 32 A.H./652-53 A.D.) was a companion of the Prophet and an early Muslim — he is claimed to have been the fifth (even the fourth) believer. He was noted for humility and asceticism. He was very religious and eager for knowledge, and is said to have matched Ibn Mas'ūd in religious learning. He was a prolific transmitter of Tradition. See Ibn Ḥajar, *op. cit.*, IV, 63ff.; Ibn 'Abd al-Barr, *op. cit.*, IV, 62-65.

This Book of Mine [i.e. the Torah] I have sent down to you; look and see how detailed I have made the explanation of My speech in it for your sake and how repeatedly have I explained things in it in order that you may reflect on its length and breadth [i.e. everything that is mentioned in it]. Despite all this you have turned away from it. Am I lighter to you than your friend? O Man, [sometimes] a certain friend of yours sits beside you; you come forth to him with your entire being and are attentive to his words wholeheartedly; if anyone talks to you or keeps you from listening to his words, you ask [that he] desists. Here I am! I have come forth to you and have talked to you, but you have kept away from Me with your mind! Have you made Me lighter than your friend?"[66]

[66] This passage of the Torah al-Ghazālī has quoted from al-Makkī's *Qūt,* I, 123 where it occurs in its entirety. Al-Makkī states (*ibid.*) that he read this passage in the Torah.

CHAPTER TWO

EXTERNAL RULES OF QUR'AN-RECITATION

لا يمسه الا المطهرون.— قرأن ٧٩:٥٦
Only those who are clean can touch the Qur'an. — Qur'an 56 : 79

ورتل القرأن ترتيلا.— قرأن ٤:٩٣
Recite the Qur'an in a slow and distinct manner. — Qur'an 93 : 4

من لم يتغن بالقران فليس منا
One who does not chant with the Qur'an is not one of us. — prophet Muḥammad

اقرءواالقرأن وابكوا، فان لم تبكوا فتباكوا
Read the Qur'an and weep. If you do not weep naturally, force yourselves to weep. — prophet Muḥammad

The external rules of Qur'an-recitation are ten in number. [These rules together with a full illustration of them are as follows]:

[I]

The first rule concerns the condition of the Qur'an-reciter.

It consists in the Qur'an-reader's being [67] in a state of ritual ablution (*waḍū'*),[68] politeness and quietness, either standing or sitting, facing the *qibla* (i.e. the direction of the Ka'ba[69] in Mecca), with the head cast down, neither sitting cross-legged nor leaning against anything nor sitting in a haughty manner. He should sit as he would when sitting in front of his teacher.

Of all the conditions [of the Qur'an-reader] the best is that he reads the Qur'an during ritual prayer standing and inside a mosque.[70] This is one of the most excellent acts of man. If,

67 واقعا(ZE: واقفا).

68 For details of ablution see Muhammad AbulQuasem, *Salvation of the Soul and Islamic Devotions,* chap. I, sec. i(forthcoming).

69 The Holy Ka'ba is the house ascribed to God (*bayt Allāh*) standing, under the sky, in the open courtyard of the Sacred Mosque (*al-Masjid al-Ḥarām*) in Mecca. In Islam the direction of the Ka'ba is the best of all directions. In some devotional acts facing the Ka'ba is a stipulation for their validity, while in others this is only praiseworthy.

70 The mosque is the best of all places on the earth. The Prophet said, "The parts of

however, he reads it without ritual ablution while reclining on his side on a bed, he has also excellence, but this excellence is of a lower grade.

[The proofs for these views are as follows:] God (exalted is He!) said, "[People of understanding are] those who remember God standing, sitting and lying on their sides, and ponder over the creation of the heavens and the earth" (الذين يذكرون الله قياما وقعودا وعلى جنوبهم، ويتفكرون فى خلق السموات والارض).[71] Thus God has praised all three conditions; He has, however, mentioned first the condition of standing in remembrance of God, then the condition of sitting and then the remembrance of God lying on one's side. 'Alī (may God be pleased with him!) said, "One who reads the Qur'an standing in ritual prayer will obtain [from God the reward of] one hundred good deeds for reading each letter of it. One who reads the Qur'an sitting in ritual prayer will obtain [the reward of] fifty good deeds for reading each letter. One who reads the Qur'an outside ritual prayer but being in a state of ritual ablution will obtain [the reward of] twenty-five good deeds. One who reads the Qur'an being without ritual ablution will obtain [the reward of] ten goods deeds."

That reading of the Qur'an which constitutes part of keeping vigil at night (*qiyām bi l-layl*) is more excellent [than reading it during daytime] for at night the mind is most free [from other matters]. Abū Dharr al-Ghifārī (may God by pleased with him!) said, "In daytime many prostrations, and at night keeping vigil for a long while are the most excellent."

[2]

The second rule concerns the amount of Qur'an-reading.

Qur'an-readers have formed different habits of considering how much they read. Some of them read the entire Qur'an right through in a day and night, some do this twice, and some even go so far as to do this thrice. Some Qur'an-readers read the Qur'an in its entirety once in a month.

The best thing in determining how much of the Qur'an to read is to rely upon the words of God's Messenger (may God bless him and greet him!), "One who has read the [entire] Qur'ran in less than

the land dearest to God are its mosques, and the parts most hateful to God are its markets." See Muslim, *Ṣaḥīḥ*, Masājid, 288.

[71] Qur'an 3:191.

three days has not understood it."[72] This is because swift reading prevents the reader from reading in a slow and distinct manner (*tartīl*).[73] When 'Ā'isha[74] [275] (may God be pleased with her!) heard a man simply babbling over the Qur'an she remarked, "This man has neither read the Qur'an nor kept silent."

The Prophet (may God bless him and greet him!) ordered 'Abd Allāh Ibn 'Umar (may God be pleased with them both!) to read the entire Qur'an once in every seven days. Likewise, a group of the Prophet's companions (may God be pleased with them!) used to complete the reading of the entire Qur'an on every Friday.[75] This group consisted of such Companions as 'Uthmān,[76] Zayd Ibn Thābit,[77] Ibn Mas'ūd, and Ubayy Ibn Ka'b[78] (may God be pleased with them!).

There are, then, four grades of the reading of the Qur'an in its entirety: [a] To read the entire Qur'an once in a day and a night. A

72 At-Tirmidhī, *Sunan*, Qur'an, 11; Abū Dāwūd, *Sunan*, Ramaḍān, 8, 9; Ibn Māja, *Sunan*, Iqāma, 178. For the concept of Qur'an-reading in order to understand its meaning see *infra*, pp. 62-65.

73 See *infra*, p. 41, n. 97.For details of Qur'an-reading in a slow and distinct manner see *infra*, pp. 41-43.

74 'Ā'isha bint Abī Bakr (d. 58 A.H./678 A.D.) was a favourite wife of the Prophet. She has the title of "mother of the believers" (Qur'an 33:6). She was a model of piety, and a prolific narrator of Tradition. She was noted for her knowledge of Arab poetry and ability to quote it, and also for her eloquence. She was well versed in Arab history and other subjects. See Watt, " 'Ā'isha bint Abī Bakr," *EI*², I, 307-308.

75 Friday is selected because it is considered in Islam to be the best of all days of the week. The blessedness of this day adds to the excellence of a pious act performed on it.

76 'Uthmān Ibn 'Affān (d. 35 A.H.), who was one of the greatest companions of the Prophet and his son-in-law, became the third caliph of Islam. A rich man, he spent a great part of his wealth for the welfare of Islam during the Prophet's lifetime. He suffered martyrdom. For an account of him see Ibn Ḥajar, *op. cit.*, II, 455f; Ibn Qutayba, *op. cit.*, pp. 191-202.

77 Zayd Ibn Thābit al-Anṣārī (d. 45 A.H.), a companion of the Prophet, is best known through his part in the codification of the Qur'an during the caliphate of Abū Bakr. A scribe of the Prophet, he recorded part of the revelations. His quickness of understanding, his sagacity and his knowledge are praised by his contemporaries. He was a specialist in the subject of hereditary law. See Ibn Ḥajar, *op. cit.*, I, 543f.; Ibn 'Abd al-Barr, *op. cit.*, I, 532ff.; Ibn Qutayba, *op. cit.*, p. 260.

78 Ubayy Ibn Ka'b (d. 22 or 30 A.H.) was a companion of the Prophet and a famous Qur'an-reader. Ibn 'Abbās studied Qur'an-reading under him. See Ibn Qutayba, *op. cit.*, p. 261; Shams ad-Dīn al-Jazarī, *Ghāya an-Nihāya fī Ṭabaqāt al-Qurrā'*, ed. Gotthelf Bergstrasser, Cairo, 1933, I, 31-32.

group [of religious scholars] has disliked this. [b] Reading the entire Qur'an [once] in every month — by reading every day one of its thirty parts. This seems to be an excessive reduction in the amount of reading, just as the first grade is an excess in over-reading. [c — d] Between these two grades are two moderate grades one of which consists in reading the entire Qur'an once in a week, and the other in reading it twice [or] nearly thrice in a week. [If twice a week] it is preferable to complete one reading of the entire Qur'an at night and the other at daytime. One should complete the reading at daytime on Monday in the two [obligatory] *rak'as* of the Dawn Prayer[79] or after them, and the reading at night on Friday night in the first two [obligatory] *rak'as* of the Sunset Prayer[80] or after them. [This is the most preferable] because it welcomes the first part of the day and of the night with the completion of Qur'an-reading. The angels (may peace be upon them!) bless the Qur'an-reader until dawn, if his completion of Qur'an-reading occurs at night, and until evening, if it[81] occurs during the daytime; thus the blessings of the two readings prevail throughout the day and throughout the night.

Details concerning the amount of Qur'an-reading are as follows. If the Qur'an-reader is one of the devotees traversing the ṣūfī path by performing good acts of the body (*al-'ābidūn as-sālikūn ṭarīq al-'amal*)[82] he should not do less than read the entire Qur'an twice a week. But if the reader is one of those who are traversing the ṣūfī path by performing actions of the soul (*as-sālikūn bi a'māl al-qalb*)[83] and by different types of reflection, or one of those who are engaged in spreading [useful] knowledge, then there is nothing wrong in reducing the reading of the entire Qur'an to once a week. If

79 The Dawn Prayer (*Ṣalāt al-Fajr*) consists of four *rak'as*, of which the first two are emphasized sunna (*sunna mu'akkada*) and the remaining two obligatory.

80 The Sunset Prayer (*Ṣalāt al-Maghrib*) consists of seven *rak'as*: the first three *rak'as* are obligatory; the next two are emphasized sunna, and the last two are supererogatory (*nafl*).

81 كانت (BE: كان).

82 Good acts of the body, i.e. acts performed by using bodily limbs, are ritual prayer, pligrimage to Mecca, Qur'an-recitation, mention of the divine name, invocation to God, and so on. Actions of the soul include remembrance of God and meditation. At a certain stage of traversing the path to God (*aṭ-ṭarīq ilā Allāh*) the novice (*sālik*) may confine himself to the performance of bodily acts, while at another stage he may concentrate on mental acts.

83 ZE has لاعمال.

the Qur'an-reader is making penetrating reflections on different meanings of the Qur'an it is sufficient for him to complete its reading once in a month, since he is much in need of repeating [the reading of verses] and reflecting [on them] many times.

[3]

The third rule concerns the mode of dividing the Qur'an [into several parts for the convenience of recitation].

As for him who [intends to] read the entire Qur'an once in a week, he will divide it into seven divisions (*aḥzāb*).

The companions of the Prophet (may God be pleased with them!) certainly divided the Qur'an into several divisions [for facilitating its recitation].[84] Thus it is related that 'Uthmān (may God be pleased with him!) used to read the Qur'an from the Sura of the Cow (*al-Baqara*) and reach the Sura of the Table (*al-Mā'ida*) on Friday night, from the Sura of Cattle (*al-An'ām*) to the Sura of Hūd on Saturday night, from the Sura of Joseph (Yūsuf) to the Sura of Mary (Maryam) on Sunday night, from the Sura of *Ṭā Hā* to the Sura of *Ṭā Sīn Mīm,* Moses (Mūsā) and Pharaoh (Fir'awn) on Monday night, from the Sura of the Spider (*al-'Ankabūt*) to the Sura of *Ṣād* on Tuesday night, from the Sura of Progressive Revelation (*Tanzīl*) to the Sura of the Most Gracious (*ar-Raḥmān*) on Wednesday night, and he used to complete the reading on Thursday night. Ibn Mas'ūd used to divide the Qur'an [into seven parts] but not in this order. It is said that the divisions of the Qur'an are seven in number: The first consists of three suras, the second of five suras, the third of seven suras, the fourth of nine suras, the fifth of eleven suras, the sixth of thirteen suras, and the seventh which is known as *al-mufaṣṣal* (divided into several pieces) starts from the Sura of *Qāf* and ends with the end of the Qur'an.

This is how the Prophet's companions (may God be pleased with them!) divided the Qur'an [for the convenience of reading], and they used to read it accordingly. On this theme is to be found a Tradition related from the Messenger of God (may God bless him and greet him!).[85] This [i.e. the division of the Qur'an into seven parts] is

[84] Ibn Māja, *Sunan*, Iqāma, 178; Abū Dāwūd, *Sunan*, Ramaḍān, 9; Ibn Ḥanbal, *Musnad*, IV, 9.

[85] Ibn Māja, *Sunan*, Iqāma, 178; Abū Dāwūd, *Sunan*, Ramaḍān, 9; Ibn Ḥanbal, *Musnad*, IV, 9, 353-55, 381, 383.

prior to the execution of its division into five parts, ten parts, and [thirty] parts. Any division other than this is something newly introduced (*muḥdath*).

[4]

The fourth rule concerns the writing of the Qur'an.

It is praiseworthy to make the writing of the Qur'an beautiful and to make its [letters] clear and distinct. There is no sin in dotting letters and writing different marks with red and other colours, because these colours adorn the Qur'an, make its [letters] distinct, and avert its reader from making mistakes and incorrect reading.

Al-Ḥasan and Ibn Sīrīn,[86] however, used to disapprove of division of the Qur'an into fifths, tenths and thirtieth parts. It is related that ash-Sha'bī[87] and Ibrāhīm[88] disliked the dotting of letters with red colour and the taking of a salary for this job. They used to say, "Keep the Qur'an free [of any superfluous things]." Concerning these scholars our conjecture is that they disliked the opening of this door, fearing that it would lead to the creation of superfluous things [in the Qur'an]. They wanted to close this door completely, and encourage the protection of the Qur'an from any change that may penetrate into it. Since the opening of this door has not in practice led to any forbidden thing, and since it has been established by the Islamic community that it is something by which added acquaintance [with the Qur'an] may be achieved, there is no

86 Muḥammad Ibn Sīrīn (d. 110 A.H./728 A.D.), a Follower, was the first renowned Muslim interpreter of dreams. He was also a great Traditionist, a jurist and an ascetic of Basra. As a Traditionist he acted more seriously than as an interpreter of dreams, although it is as the latter that he finally came to be well known. See an-Nawawī, *Tahdhīb al-Asmā' wa l-Lughāt*, Egypt, n.d., I. 82ff.; T. Fahd, "Ibn Sīrīn", *EI*², III, 947-48.

87 Abū 'Amr 'Āmir ash-Sha'bī (d. 104 or 105 A.H.) was a prominent and trustworthy Traditionist who heard Traditions from more than five hundred companions of the Prophet. Like his father Sharaḥbīl, he was one of the foremost of "Qur'an-readers" of Kufa. A great learned man, he was often consulted by the jurists in Kufa on legal matters. Among his many pupils was Imām Abū Ḥanīfa. He had an inexhaustable knowledge of poetry and an extremely sharp memory. See Ibn Qutayba, *op. cit.*, pp. 449-51.

88 Ibrāhīm Ibn Yazīd an-Nakha'ī (d. 96 A.H./714-15 A.D.), a Follower, was a great authority on jurisprudence and a scholar of Tradition. See Ibn Qutayba, *op. cit.*, pp. 463f.; an-Nawawī, *op. cit.*, I, 104f.

sin in it. The fact that it is a new thing introduced in Islam (*muhdath*) does not mean that it should be forbidden, for many a newly introduced thing is good. For example, concerning the establishment of congregation (*jamā'a*) in the case of *Tarāwīḥ* Prayer[89] it is said that it is one of the practices newly introduced in Islam by 'Umar[90] (may God be pleased with him!) but that it is a good innovation (*bid'a ḥasana*). A condemnable innovation (*bid'a madhmūma*) is only that which opposes an old established sunna (*as-sunna al-qadīma*) or which tends to bring about a change in it.[91]

A certain religious scholar used to say, "I shall read from the *muṣḥaf* in which letters are dotted, but shall not dot them myself."

Awza'ī[92] said, on the authority of Yaḥyā Ibn Abī Kathīr,[93] "The Qur'an was kept free [of dots, marks, and so on] in *muṣḥaf*. The

[89] This ritual prayer is performed after the Evening Prayer (*Ṣalāt al-'Ishā'*) in the lunar month of Ramaḍān. It is an emphasized sunna prayer for both men and women. Performance of this ritual prayer in congregation is a collective sunna (*sunna kifāya*) so that its performance by some people of a locality in congregation while by others alone is sufficient. For details about the time, number of *rak'as* and the methods of the performance of this ritual prayer see Quasem, *Salvation*, chap. II, sec. xxvi.

[90] 'Umar Ibn al-Khaṭṭāb (d. 23 A.H.). Of all the companions of the Prophet, 'Umar was the most intimate to him after Abū Bakr. For the strength of his faith, firmness of his mind and his acute sense of justice the Prophet once remarked: Satan flees away from the path along which 'Umar walks. His service to Islam during the lifetimes of the Prophet and Abū Bakr was great. He succeeded Abū Bakr and in the ten years of his caliphate rendered tremendous services to Islam — its propagation, territorial expansion, and administration. He is buried by the side of the graves of the Prophet and Abū Bakr. See Ibn Hajar *op. cit.*, II, 511f.; Ibn Qutayba, *op. cit.*, pp. 179-190; Ibn 'Abd al-Barr, *op. cit.*, II, 450-66.

[91] This is the definition of a condemnable innovation concerning action. Regarding belief (*i'tiqād*) also, condemnable innovations have come into existence. Al-Ghazālī has explained (*Iḥyā'*, IV, 175) how a heretic is in great danger of losing his faith.

[92] 'Abd ar-Raḥmān al-Awza'ī (d. 157 A.H./774 A.D.) was the main representative of the ancient Syrian school of Islamic jurisprudence. He was often quoted by subsequent jurists, such as Abū Yūsuf and ash-Shāfi'ī. He had a number of prominent disciples. The ancient school of the Syrians transformed itself into the personal school (*madhhab*) of al-Awza'ī. It prevailed not only in Syria but also in the Maghrib, including Islamic Spain, before it was superseded by the school (*madhhab*) of Imām Mālik, See J. Schacht, "Al-Awza'ī, "*EI*^{2}, I, 272-73; Ibn Qutayba, *op. cit.*, pp. 496f.

[93] Abū Naṣr Yaḥyā Ibn Abī Kāthīr al-Yamāmī (d. 129 A.H.), a Follower, was a devotee (*'ābid*) and a Traditionist who narrated Traditions from several companions of the Prophet. See 'Abd ar-Ra'ūf al-Munāwī, *al-Kawākib ad-Durriyya*, ed. by Maḥmūd Ḥasan Rabī', Cairo, 1938/1357, I, 180.

first thing people have introduced in it is the dotting at the letter *bā* (ب) and the letter *tā* (ت), maintaining [276] that there is no sin in this, for this illuminates the Qur'an. After this people have introduced big dots at the end of verses, maintaining that there is no sin in this, for by this the beginning of a verse can be known. After this people introduced marks showing the ends of suras (*khawātīm*) and marks showing their beginnings (*fawātiḥ*).

Abū Bakr al-Hadhlī[94] said, "I asked al-Ḥasan concerning the dotting of *muṣḥafs* with red colour. He enquired, 'What is the dotting of them? I replied, 'People place vowel marks according to the grammatical rules of Arabic.' He said, 'As for the desinential syntax (*i'rāb*) of the Qur'an, there is no sin in it.' " Khālid al-Ḥidhdhā'[95] said, "I visited Ibn Sīrīn and saw him reading from a dotted *muṣḥaf*. He of course used to dislike dots."

It is said that Ḥajjāj[96] is the one who introduced the system [of dotting, marking and so on in the Qur'an]: He brought the Qur'an-readers [of Basra and Kufa] to his court, and they enumerated words of the Qur'an, [its verses] and its letters, made its parts equal, and divided it into thirty parts and into other parts [such as fifths and tenths].

[5]

The fifth rule is to read the Qur'an in a slow and distinct manner (*tartīl*).[97]

This manner of reading is praiseworthy (*mustaḥab*) in the case of the Qur'an because, as we shall soon discuss,[98] the purpose of

[94] Abū Bakr Salmān (or Rūḥ) al-Hadhlī (d. 197 A.H.) was a Follower and a Traditionist who narrated Traditions on the authority of al-Ḥasan, ash-Sha'bī, and on whose authority Abū Nu'aym and Muslim Ibn Ibrāhim narrated Traditions. See az-Zabīdī, *op. cit.*, IV, 477.

[95] Khālid Ibn Mihrān al-Ḥidhdhā' (d. 141 A.H.) was a leading, trustworthy Traditionist, See *ibid.*; Ibn Qutayba, *op. cit.*, p. 501.

[96] Ḥajjāj Ibn Yūsuf ath-Thaqafī (d. 95 A.H./714 A.D.) was the most famous and the ablest governor of the Umayyads. The method which made him famous was indeed notorious — extreme severity, atrocities and bloodshed far more than was necessary. He shed blood even in the Holy city of Mecca and bombarded the Holy Ka'ba and the pilgrims there. He, however, did a few good things, one of which was the division of the Qur'an into separate parts and the introduction of vowel points in it. See Ibn Qutayba, *op. cit.*, p. 548.

[97] This is commanded in the Qur'anic verse (73:4), "Recite the Qur'an in a slow and distinct manner."

[98] See *infra*, pp. 62-5.

reading the Qur'an is reflection [on its meaning] (*tafakkur*), and reading in a slow and distinct manner assists this. For this reason Umm Salama[99] (may God be pleased with her!) described the Qur'an-reading of the Messenger of God (may God bless him and greet him!), when she was asked concerning it; immediately [after being asked] she began to describe its recitation as clear and distinct in respect of every letter.[100] 'Abd Allāh Ibn 'Abbās[101] (may God be pleased with them both!) said, "That I read the Sura of the Cow (*al-Baqara*)[102] and the Sura of the House of 'Imrān (*Āl 'Imrān*)[103] in a slow and distinct manner while pondering over them, is better for me than to read the entire[104] Qur'an babbling." He also said, "That I read [the sura beginning with] 'When the earth is shaken (*idhā zulzilat*)[105] and the Sura of the Clatterer (*al-Qāri'a*)[106], reflecting over them, is better for me than to read the Sura of the Cow and the Sura of the House of 'Imrān babbling." Mujāhid[107] was asked concerning two men who started ritual prayer and who

99 Umm Salama (d. 59 A.H.) was a wife of the Prophet. She has the title of "mother of the believers" (Qur'an 33:6). The Prophet married her in 4 A.H. She died one year and several days after the death of 'Ā'isha. See Ibn Ḥajar, *op. cit.*, IV, 439ff.; Ibn 'Abd al-Barr, *op. cit.*, IV, 436f.

100 An-Nasā'ī, *Sunan*, Iftitāḥ, 83, Qiyām al-layl, 13; at-Tirmidhī, *Sunan*, Thawāb al-Qur'an 23; Ibn Ḥanbal, *Musnad*, VI, 30, 294.

101 'Abd Allāh Ibn 'Abbās (d. 68 A.H.) was a cousin and a great companion of the Prophet. In the early period of Islam he was called 'the learned man of Islamic community.' He is also called 'the leader of the exegetes of the Qur'an.' See Ibn Ḥajar, *op. cit.*, II, 322-26.

102 This is the second sura of the Qur'an consisting of two hundred and eighty-six verses. The Verse of the Throne (*Āyat al-Kursī*) is included in it.

103 This is the third Qur'anic sura consisting of two hundred verses.

104 كلّه is omitted in BE.

105 This is the ninety-ninth sura of the Qur'an consisting of only eight verses which deal with the Day of Resurrection and the consequences of man's actions. There is a Tradition (Ibn Ḥanbal, *Musnad*, III, 148, 221) that this sura is equal to a fourth part of the Qur'an in respect of value.

106 This is the one hundred and first sura consisting of only eleven verses which speak of the Doomsday, the weighing of man's actions in the Balance and their consequences in the form of happiness in Paradise or punishment in Hell.

107 Mujāhid Ibn Jubayr (d. 100 or 101 or 102 or 103 A.H.), a great Follower and a disciple of Ibn 'Abbās, was an authority on Qur'anic exegesis. His opinions on this subject are often quoted by subsequent writers on the Qur'an, such as al-Ghazālī and al-Makkī. He was also a scholar of jurisprudence and Tradition. He died while in prostration before God. See Ibn Qutayba, *op. cit.*, pp. 444f.; an-Nawawī, *op. cit.*, II, 83.

stood in that prayer for the same duration, but one of whom read only the Sura of the Cow and the other the Qur'an in its entirety. He replied, "They are equal in respect of merit."

Know that reading the Qur'an in a slow and distinct manner is praiseworthy not merely because it assists pondering (*tadabbur*) over it, since for a non-Arab (*'ajamī*) who does not understand the meaning of the Qur'an it is also praiseworthy to read it in a slow and distinct manner with pauses between the sentences, because this is nearer to the reverence and respect [which the Qur'an deserves] and stronger in its impression on the soul than babbling with haste.

[6]

The sixth rule is weeping [while reading the Qur'an].

Weeping while reading the Qur'an is praiseworthy (*mustaḥab*). The Messenger of God (may God bless him and greet him!) commanded, "Recite the Qur'an and weep. If you do not weep naturally, then force yourself to weep."[108] The Prophet (may God bless him and greet him!) declared, "One who does not chant with the Qur'an is not one of us."[109] Ṣāliḥ al-Murrī[110] said, "I read the Qur'an to the Messenger of God (may God bless him and greet him!) in my sleep. He asked me, 'Ṣāliḥ, this is only the reading of the Qur'an, but where is the weeping?' " 'Abd Allāh Ibn 'Abbās (may God be pleased with them both!) said, "When you read [the Qur'anic verse of] prostration in which occurs the word *subḥāna*,[111] do not hasten to prostrate until you weep. If the eyes of anyone of you do not weep his mind should weep [i.e. be filled with grief and fear of God]."

The method of forcing oneself to weep consists in bringing grief to the mind. From this grief will be produced weeping. The Prophet (may God bless him and greet him!) said, "Surely the Qur'an was revealed with grief. So when you read it you should force yourself to

108 Ibn Māja, *Sunan*, Iqāma, 176, Zuhd, 19. In the Qur'an (17:109) also weeping is praised. The Prophet himself was seen weeping at Qur'an-recitation. See *infra*, n. 151.

109 Al-Bukhārī, *Ṣaḥīḥ*, Tawḥīd, 44; Ibn Ḥanbal, *Musnad*, I, 172, 175, 179; ad-Dārimī, *Sunan*, Ṣalā, 171, Faḍā'il al-Qur'an, 34.

110 Ṣāliḥ al-Murrī (d. 178 A.H.) was a famous ascetic of Basra. He was also a preacher and a Traditionist. See az-Zabīdī, *op. cit.*, I, 199, IV, 479.

111 Qur'an 17:107-109. For details of prostration due to Qur'an-reading see *infra*, pp. 44-7; Quasem, *Salvation*, chap. II, see. xxxv.

be aggrieved." The method of bringing grief [to the mind] of the Qur'an-reader is through reflecting on the threats, warnings, covenants and promises which are contained in the Qur'an. Then he will reflect on his shortcomings in respect of the commandments of the Qur'an and its threats [of punishment]. Thus he will necessarily be aggrieved and will weep. Should he not feel grief and weep as do those who have purified souls, he should weep for his lack of grief and tears, because this is the greatest of all misfortunes.

[7]

The seventh rule is to fulfil the right (*ḥaqq*) of the Qur'anic verses recited.

Thus when the Qur'an-reader reads a verse necessitating prostration before God he will prostrate himself. Likewise, if he hears [the recitation of] a verse of prostration by another person he will prostrate himself when the reciter prostrates. He will prostrate only when he is physically and ritually clean.[112] There are fourteen verses of prostration in the Qur'an.[113] In the Sura of Pilgrimage (*al-Ḥajj*) there are two verses of prostration.[114] There is no verse of prostration in the Sura of *Ṣād*.[115]

The minimum requirement of prostration [due to Qur'an-reading] is that the prostrater prostrates by putting his forehead on the ground, [without uttering *Allāhu akbar* (الله اكبر or God is the greatest) and without any supplication]. Its perfect form is for him to utter *Allāhu akbar* and then prostrate himself and, while prostrate, supplicate with that supplication which is appropriate to the verse of prostration recited. For example, if he has read the

[112] The problem of cleanliness, physical and ritual, is discussed in great detail in Quasem, *Salvation*, chap. I.

[113] According to the Ḥanafī school (*madhhab*) of Islamic jurisprudence, these verses are: 7:206, 13:15, 16:49, 17:107, 19:58, 22:18, 25:60, 27:25, 32:15, 38:39, 41:37, 55:62, 84:21, 96:19. This is recorded in the *muṣḥaf* of 'Uthmān, and is the reliable view.

[114] This view of al-Ghazālī agrees with that of the Shāfi'ī and Ḥanbalī schools of jurisprudence. According to the Ḥanafī school, however, there is only one verse of prostration (22:18) in the Sura of Pilgrimage, the twenty-second sura of the Qur'an. See az-Zabīdī, *op. cit.*, IV, 480-81.

[115] This view of al-Ghazālī, like that of some other jurists, disagrees with the opinion of the Ḥanafī school which affirms the existence of a verse of prostration (38:34) in the Sura of Ṣād, the thirty-eighth sura of the Qur'an.

words of God (exalted is He!), "They fall down prostrate and celebrate the praise of their Lord and are not arrogant" (خروا سجدا، وسبحوا بحمد ربهم،وهم لا يستكبرون),[116] he will supplicate:

> God, make me one of those who prostrate themselves before You for Your pleasure and who glorify You with Your praise. I seek Your protection from being one of those who are arrogant against Your command or against Your friends [i.e. saints].
>
> (اللهم، اجعلنى من الساجدين لوجهك، المسبحين بحمدك. واعوذبك ان اكون من المستكبرين عن امرك، اوعلى اوليائك).
>
> (*Allāhumma, aj'alnī min as-sājidīna li-wajhika, al-musabbiḥīna bi-ḥamdika. Wa a'ūdhu bi-ka, 'an akūna min al-mustakbirīna 'an amrika, aw 'alā awliyā'ika*).

On reading the words of God (exalted is He!), "They weep while they prostrate themselves, and this adds to their humility" (ويخرون للاذقان يبكون، ويزيدهم خشوعا),[117] the Qur'an-reader will supplicate:

> God, make me one of those who weep for fear of You, and who are humble towards You.
>
> (اللهم، اجعلنى من الباكين اليك، الخاشعين لك)
>
> (*Allāhumma, aj'alnī min al-bākīna ilayka, al-khāshi'īna laka*).

In this way the Qur'an-reader will supplicate while making every prostration [due to his reading or hearing a verse of prostration].

In the case of prostration due to Qur'an-reading it is necessary to fulfil those stipulations which are meant for ritual prayer (*shurūṭ aṣ-ṣalā*), such as covering one's private parts (*satr al-'awra*),[118] facing the *qibla* (i.e. the direction of the Ka'ba[119] in Mecca), and cleanliness of clothing and body against ritual impurity (*ḥadath*) and physical filth (*khubuth*).[120] A man who is not clean when

116 Qur'an 32:15. 117 Qur'an 17:109.

118 The legal definition of private parts is as follows: In the case of a man, whether free or slave, they are that part of the body which lies between his navel and the end of his knees. In the case of a slave woman her belly and back are also included. For a free woman the private parts are her entire body except the face, the palms together with the back of the hands, and the feet, both their inward and outward sides. See Ḥasan Ibn 'Ammār ash-Shurunbalālī, *Matn Nūr al-Īḍāḥ*, Cairo, 1389/1969, p. 43.

119 See *supra*, n. 69.

120 For details about cleanliness see Quasem, *Salvation*, chap. I.

hearing [the recitation of a verse of prostration by another man], will prostrate when he becomes clean.

It is said that, in the perfect form of prostration due to Qur'an-reading, the prostrater will utter *Allāhu akbar*, lifting his hands [level with his shoulders], thereby making all other things unlawful to himself.[121] Then he will again utter *Allāhu akbar* while inclining towards prostration. [Then he will prostrate himself]. Then he will utter *Allāhu akbar* while lifting the head [from prostration], and then will make the salutation [to the right and to the left as he withdraws from prostration]. Some authorities have added [277] to this the reading of the formula of Witnessing (*at-tashahhud*).[122] There is no basis for these views except an analogy (*qiyās*) with the prostration of ritual prayer. This analogy, however, is far [from being sound], because what has occurred [in the Qur'an] is only the command of prostration, and so this command should be obeyed [by prostration only]. The utterance of *Allāhu akbar* while inclining towards prostration is nearer to the beginning [and so this should be done]; all other things are far [from what can be supported by Islamic jurisprudence].

The follower of the *imām*,[123] [in a ritual prayer performed in

121 In legal terminology this is called *taḥrīma*, i.e. that by which every irrelevant act becomes unlawful to the devotee. It is necessary at the start of all kinds of ritual prayer.

122 This is the formula read at the end of the second and the fourth *rak'a* of a ritual prayer. It is also read at the end of the third *rak'a* if the ritual prayer is of only three *rak'as*. The Ḥanafī school of jurisprudence prescribes the Witnessing of 'Abd Allāh Ibn Mas'ūd — the Witnessing which the Prophet taught him. The Shāfi'ī school, however, prescribes a different Witnessing.

123 *Imām* (leader) in this context means the man who leads a group of people in a ritual prayer. He will be granted a great reward on the Day of Judgement should he lead the prayer to the satisfaction of the congregation. See *supra*, n. 26. Performance of ritual prayer in congregation is very meritorious and is emphasized in the Qur'an (62:9) and the Sunna. The Prophet declared, "A ritual prayer in congregation is twenty-seven times more excellent than a ritual prayer performed by a single person" (al-Bukhārī, *Ṣaḥīḥ*, adhān, 29; Muslim, *Ṣaḥīḥ*, Masājid, 245, 247). Once when some people remained absent from a certain ritual prayer in congregation the Prophet warned: "I intended to order a man to lead the ritual prayer and myself go to those who did not attend it and burn their houses" (al-Bukhārī, *Ṣaḥīḥ*, Adhān, 29; an-Nasā'ī, *Sunan*, Imāma, 49; Ibn Māja, *Sunan*, Masājid, 17). Despite this stress of the Prophet the Shī'as do not perform ritual prayer in congregation. What has led them to this is their view on *imāma*, leadership of the Islamic community. For details of ritual prayer in congregation see Quasem, *Salvation*, chap. II, sec. xi.

congregation], should prostrate himself when his *imām* prostrates. A man, if he be a follower (*ma'mūm*) of an *imām*, will not prostrate himself because of his own recitation [of a verse of prostration].[124]

[8]

The eighth rule [concerns supplication before, after and during the Qur'an-reading]. At the start of his Qur'an-reading,[125] the Qur'an-reader will supplicate:

> I seek the protection of God, the All-hearing, the All-knowing, against the rejected Satan. 'Lord, I seek refuge with You from the incitements of Satans, and I seek refuge with You, Lord, lest they should approach me.'[126]
> (اعوذ بالله السميع العليم من الشيطان الرجيم. رب، اعوذبك من همزات الشياطين، واعوذبك رب ان يحضرون)
> ***(A'ūdhu bi-Allāhi as-samī'i al-'alīmi, min ash-Shayṭāni ar-rajīmi. 'Rabbi, a'ūdhu bika min hamazāti ash-Shayāṭīni, wa a'udhu bika rabbi 'an yaḥḍurūni').***

He should also supplicate by reading [the sura which starts with] "Proclaim: I seek the protection of the Lord of mankind" (قل اعوذ برب الناس)[127] and [the sura which starts with] "Praise be to God!"(الحمد لله).[128]

On completion of Qur'an-reading, the Qur'an-reader should supplicate:

> God (exalted is He!) has spoken the truth, and His Messenger (may God bless him and greet him!) has con-

124 For more details of prostration due to one's reading or hearing a Qur'anic verse of prostration see Quasem, *Salvation*, chap. II, sec. xxxv.

125 Qur'an 16:98 — "When you read the Qur'an, seek the protection of God against Satan, the rejected."

126 Qur'an 23:97.

127 This is the hundred and fourteenth sura of the Qur'an consisting of only six short verses. This and its preceding sura are together known as the *Mu'awwidhatān* (the suras of taking refuge with God) and are the best protective formulae to ward off evil, especially demonic suggestions. The practice of taking refuge with God is commanded at various points in the Qur'an. See az-Zabīdī, *op. cit.*, IV, 491.

128 This is the Opening Sura of the Qur'an consisting of only seven short verses which contain the gist of all Qur'anic verses and which constitute the key to all seven doors of Paradise. This sura is distinguished as the best of all Qur'anic suras. See Quasem, *Jewels*, chaps. XII, XIII, XVII.

veyed [it to us]. God, benefit us with the Qur'an and bless us in it. Praise be to God, the Lord of all the worlds! I seek the forgiveness of God, the Ever Living, the Self-subsisting and All-sustaining.

(صدق الله تعالى، وبلغ رسول الله صلى الله عليه وسلم. اللهم، انفعنا به، وبارك لنا فيه. الحمد لله رب العالمين، واستغفر الله الحى القيوم)

(*Ṣadaqa Allāhu ta'āla, wa ballagha rasūlu Allāhi, ṣalla Allāhu 'alayhi wa sallama. Allāhumma, anfa'nā bihi, wa bārik lanā fīhi. Al-ḥamdu li-Allāhi rabbi al-'ālamīna, wa astaghfiru Allāha al-ḥayya al-qayyūma*).

During the Qur'an-reading, when the Qur'an-reader reads a verse on glorification of God, he will glorify Him and magnify Him. When he reads a verse on supplication [to God] and forgiveness [of Him], he will supplicate and seek forgiveness. If he reads a verse telling of any hopeful matter he will pray to God [for it]. But if he reads a verse on a frightening matter, he will seek the protection [of God from it]. He will do these with his tongue or with his mind. Thus, [in place of glorification of God] he will say: Glory be to God! (*subḥāna Allāhi*); [in place of seeking refuge with God] he will say: We seek the protection of God (*na'ūdhu bi-Allāhi*); and [in place of making petition to God] he will say: God, grant us sustenance; God, bestow mercy upon us (*Allāhumma arzuqnā, Allāhumma arḥimnā*).

Ḥudhayfa[129] said, "Once I performed my ritual prayer behind God's (exalted is He!) Messenger (may God bless him and greet him!).[130] He started the Qur'an-reading of [that ritual prayer] with the Sura of the Cow (*Sura al-Baqara*). On reading every verse on divine mercy he prayed to God for it. On reading every verse on chastisement he sought refuge with God. On reading every verse on the purification of God (*tanzīh*) he glorified Him.[131] On completion

129 Ḥidhayfa Ibn al-Yamān (d. 36 A.H.) was a great companion of the Prophet. He took part in the battle of Uḥud and was selected by the Prophet to obtain information on the Quraysh at the battle of Ditch. He was the governor of Midian during the caliphate of 'Umar. He narrated many Traditions from the Prophet and 'Umar. He was known to the Companions as "the possessor of secret knowledge of the Prophet". He used to ask the Prophet about hidden defects of the soul, secret traits of the hypocrites, and future disturbances (*fitan*). For this reason ṣūfīs often quote his sayings on these matters. See Ibn Ḥajar *op. cit.*, I, 316f.; Ibn 'Abd al-Barr, *op. cit.*, I, 276ff.; al-Munāwī, *op. cit.*, I, 50f.

130 صلى الله عليه وسلم (BE: صلى الله تعالى عليه وعلى اله وسلم).

131 Muslim, *Ṣaḥīḥ*, Musāfirīn, 203.

of the reading of the sura he supplicated by reading that [supplication-formula] which he (may God's blessings and greetings be upon him![132] used to read on completing the reading of the entire Qur'an. [This formula is as follows:]

> God, bestow mercy upon me through the Qur'an, and make it for me a leader [who leads to the truth], a light, a guide, and a mercy. God, remind me of that which I have forgotten [when reading the Qur'an], teach me those parts of the Qur'an of which I am ignorant, grant me its recitation 'in the hours of the night and different parts of the day,'[133] and make it a point in my favour, O Lord of all the worlds."[134]
>
> (اللهم، ارحمنى بالقرأن، واجعله لى اماما ونورا وهدى ورحمة. اللهم، ذكرنى منه مانسيت، وعلمنى منه ما جهلت، وارزقنى تلاوته اناء الليل واطراف النهار. واجعله لى حجة، يا رب العالمين)
>
> (*Allāhumma, arḥimnī bi-l-Qur'āni, wa aj'alhu lī imāmān wa nūran wa hudan wa raḥmatan. Allāhumma, dhakkirnī minhu mā nasītu, wa 'allimnī minhu mā jahiltu, wa arzuqnī tilāwatahu ānā' al-layli wa aṭrāfa an-nahāri, wa aj'alhu lī ḥujjatan, yā rabba al-'ālamīna*).

[9]

The ninth rule concerns the reading of the Qur'an aloud.

There is no doubt that it is necessary to read the Qur'an loud enough so that the reader can hear it himself because reading means distinguishing clearly between sounds; thus sound is necessary, and the smallest degree of it is that which he can hear himself. If he cannot hear himself in a ritual prayer (*ṣalā*), his prayer is not correct.

As for reading so loud that he can be heard by others, it is to be considered praiseworthy in one respect and undesirable in another.

132 يقوله صلواة الله عليه وسلامه (BE: يقول صلوات الله وسلامه).

133 Qur'an 20:130.

134 It is praiseworthy (*mustaḥab*) to supplicate on completion of a reading of the Qur'an in its entirety. This supplication is received by God, and His mercy descends upon the supplicant. For these reasons the companions of the Prophet and those who followed them used to gather together the members of their families and other people to supplicate on completion of their recitations of the entire Qur'an. See az-Zabīdī, *op. cit.*, IV, 492.

The proofs that silent reading of the Qur'an is praiseworthy are [as follows]: It is related that the Prophet (may God bless him and greet him!) said, "The excellence of silent reading of the Qur'an compared with reading it aloud is like the excellence of secret almsgiving compared with public almsgiving." In other words this Tradition runs thus: "One who reads the Qur'an aloud is like one who gives alms publicly, and one who reads the Qur'an silently is like one who gives alms secretly."[135] In a generally received Tradition [one finds that the Prophet said]: "A secret good act is more excellent than a public good act by seventy times." Likewise is the saying of the Prophet (may God bless him and greet him!): "The best measure of sustenance (*rizq*) is that which is sufficient, and the best mode of invocation of God (*dhikr*) is that which is secret."[136]

In a Tradition [one finds that the Prophet warned]: "Some of you will not read the Qur'an aloud near others during the time between the Sunset Prayer (*Maghrib*) and the Evening Prayer (*'Ishā'*)."[137] One night, in the Mosque of the Messenger of God (may God bless him and greet him!), Sa'īd Ibn al-Musayyab[138] heard 'Umar Ibn 'Abd al-'Azīz[139] reading the Qur'an aloud in his ritual prayer — and he was a man of sweet voice. Sa'īd ordered his slave, "Go to this devotee and ask him to lower his voice." The slave said [to Sa'īd], "The mosque is not reserved for us only; that devotee has also a share in it." [Rejecting this argument of his slave] Sa'īd [himself] raised his voice, saying, "Devotee, if you intend to obtain the pleasure of God (great and mighty is He!) by your ritual prayer, then lower your voice. If, however, you intend to obtain the pleasure of people [you should know that] they will never be sufficient in respect

135 Abū Dāwūd, *Sunan*, Taṭawwu', 25, an-Nasā'ī, *Sunan*, Zakā, 68; at-Tirmidhī, *Sunan*, Thawāb al-Qur'an, 20; Ibn Ḥanbal, *Musnad*, IV, 151, 158, 201.

136 Ibn Ḥanbal, *Musnad*, I, 172, 180, 187.

137 Ibn Ḥanbal, *Musnad*, II, 36, 67, 129, IV, 344 (with variation).

138 Sa'īd Ibn al-Musayyab (d. 93 or 94 A.H.), a leading Follower, was the greatest jurist of the Hijaz in his time. He was also a great interpreter of dreams and a noted Traditionist who transmitted Traditions from many prominent companions of the Prophet. In knowledge and piety he was the greatest of all Followers. See an-Nawawī, *op. cit.*, I, 219ff.; Ibn Qutayba, *op. cit.*, pp. 437f.

139 'Umar Ibn 'Abd al-'Azīz (d. 101 A.H.) was a Follower and an Umayyad caliph (717-20 A.D.) who in all his affairs, personal and administrative, tried to imitate the caliph 'Umar Ibn al-Khaṭṭāb. Al-Ghazālī calls him "the greatest ascetic of his time". He had correspondences with al-Ḥasan al-Baṣrī on piety and asecticism. See al-Ghazālī, *Iḥyā'* I, 69; Ibn Qutayba, *op. cit.*, pp. 362f

of anything against God." 'Umar remained silent and shortened the *rak'a* of his ritual prayer. On salutation [to his right side and left side by which he withdrew from the ritual prayer], he took his shoes and departed. At that time he was the governor of Medina.

The proofs that reading the Qur'an aloud is praiseworthy are [as follows]: It is related that the Prophet (may God bless him and greet him!) once heard a group of his companions reading the Qur'an aloud in the supererogatory ritual prayer performed after midnight (*ṣalāt al-layl*) and approved of this.[140] The Prophet (may God bless him [278] and greet him!) [also] said, "If one of you keeps vigil at night performing supererogatory ritual prayers, he should read the Qur'an aloud, because the angels as well as those who are staying at his house listen to his Qur'an-reading and pray to God with his ritual prayer." Once the Prophet (may God bless him and greet him!) passed by three of his companions (may God be pleased with them!) who were engaged in different modes of Qur'an-reading: He passed by Abū Bakr[141] (may God be pleased with him!) who was reading the Qur'an silently. The Prophet asked him concerning the reason for this. He replied, "[I am reading silently because] the One to Whom I am whispering can hear me." The Prophet passed by 'Umar (may God be pleased with him!) who was reading the Qur'an aloud. He asked him the reason for this. 'Umar replied. "[By reading aloud] I am awakening those who are asleep and [also] threatening Satan." The Prophet passed by Bilāl[142] who was reading some verses from one sura and other verses from other suras. The Prophet asked him the reason. He replied, "I am

140 Al-Bukhārī, *Ṣaḥīḥ*, Maghāzī, 38; Muslim, *Ṣaḥīḥ*, Faḍā'il aṣ-Ṣaḥāba, 166; Abū Dāwūd, *Sunan*, Taṭawwu', 25.

141 Abū Bakr aṣ-Ṣiddīq (d. 13 A.H.) was the first of all adult male persons to accept Islam. He was a father-in-law of the Prophet and his greatest companion. As the first successor of the Prophet he served Islam for two years. His service to the cause of Islam both during and after the Prophet's lifetime was only next to that of the Prophet himself. For details see Ibn Qutayba, *op. cit.*, pp. 167-78.

142 Bilāl Ibn Abī Rabāḥ was a companion of the Prophet and is best known as his *mu'adhdhin* (one who calls to ritual prayer). He was an early convert to Islam — having been the second adult after Abū Bakr. He accompanied the Prophet on all expeditions. In addition to being his *mu'adhdhin* he was also the Prophet's 'mace-bearer', his steward, his personal servant, and, on occasions, his 'adjutant'. He attained high prestige during his lifetime. The date of his death is variously given as 17, 18, 20, or 21 A.H./638, 639, 641, or 642 A.D. For details see W. 'Arafat, "Bilāl b. Rabāḥ," *EI*^{2}, I, 1215.

mingling [some] good things with other good things." The Prophet (may God bless him and greet him!) remarked, "Everyone of you has done good and right."

The method of reconciliation among these [apparently conflicting] Traditions is that the silent reading of the Qur'an is furthest from ostentation (*riyā'*)[143] and affectation, and hence it is better [than reading aloud] in the case of a Qur'an-reader who is afraid of these for himself. If, however, he has no fear of these, and if loud reading of the Qur'an does not disturb (lit. confuse the time to) another devotee, then reading with a loud voice is better, [a] because it involves more effort, [b] because its benefit is also linked up with others — a good which involves other people is better than a good which cleaves to its agent only —, [c] because loud reading awakens the mind of the Qur'an-reader, unites his care for reflection on [the meaning of] the Qur'an and turns his ear to it, [d] because loud reading repels sleep by raising the voice, [e] because it adds to his energy for Qur'an-reading and lessens his laziness, [f] because waking a sleeping man can be expected from loud reading, in which case the Qur'an-reader will be the cause of the man's revival [from laziness which led him to sleep], and [g] because sometimes, having seen the loud reader, a workless, idle man gets energized because of his energy and encouraged to serve [God].

When one of these intentions is present loud reading of the Qur'an is better [than silent reading]. Should all these intentions join together the reward of Qur'an-reading would multiply. Because of many intentions good acts of the pious grow, and the rewards they obtain multiply. If in a single act there are ten intentions ten rewards are to be obtained from it.

For this reason we say that reading from *muṣḥafs* is better [than reading the Qur'an from memory], for, [in the former case], to the action of reading are added looking at the *muṣḥaf*, thinking about it, and carrying it; so the reward of Qur'an-reading will increase because of the addition of these. It is said that reading the entire Qur'an once from the *muṣḥaf* is equal [in value] to reading it in its

143 Ostentation is defined as the desire to please men through a devotional act. It renders the act not only void but also sinful. It is strongly prohibited in the Qur'an (4:142, 107:6, 2:264, 4:38, 8:47) and in Tradition where it is called the lesser polytheism (Ibn Ḥanbal, *Musnad*, V, 428, 429). Devotional acts must be performed only for God alone. See Qur'an 18:110.

entirety seven times from memory, because looking at a *muṣḥaf* is also an act of devotion to God (*'ibāda*). 'Uthmān (may God be pleased with him!) tore two *muṣḥafs* by reading much from them. Many Companions used to read from *muṣḥafs*, and they were unhappy when a day in which they did not look at *muṣḥafs* passed. A certain Egyption jurist (*faqīh*) visited ash-Shāfi'ī[144] (may God be pleased with him!) at dawn when he had in front of him a *muṣḥaf* [from which he was reading]. Ash-Shāfi'ī said to him, "Excessive study of jurisprudence[145] has prevented you from reading the Qur'an. [For my part] I perform the Dawn Prayer in darkness and then put the *muṣḥaf* in front of me [for reading from it]; I do not shut it until there is day-light."

[10]

The tenth rule is to read the Qur'an beautifully and in a slow and distinct manner,[146] by controlling the voice though not with that excessive stretch which changes the prose order (*naẓm*).

This is sunna. The Prophet (may God bless him and greet him!) said, "Adorn the Qur'an with your voices."[147] He (may God bless him and greet him!) [also] said, "God does not listen to anything as much as He does to man's sweet voice at Qur'an-reading."[148] He (may God bless him and greet him!) [further] said, "One who does not chant (*yataghannā*) with the Qur'an is not one of us." Some authorities have said that by the word '*yataghannā*' the Prophet meant 'to feel independent', while others have said that he meant by it 'chanting melodiously and by controlling the tones of voice'. This latter view is nearest [to the truth] in the opinion of philologists. It is related that once at night [after the Evening Prayer (*Ṣalāt al-'Ishā'*)] the Messenger of God (may God bless him and greet him!) was waiting for 'Ā'isha (may God be pleased with her!) [to come to

144 Muḥammad Ibn Idrīs ash-Shāfi'ī (d. 204 A.H.) was the founder of the Shāfi'ite school (*madhhab*) of jurisprudence. See al-Ghazālī, *Iḥyā'*, I, 24-27 where an account of his piety and devotion is given. This account is expressly based upon Shaykh Naṣr Ibn Ibrāhīm al-Maqdisī's work on the good traits of Imām Shāfi'ī.

145 الفقه (BE: الفكر).

146 Qur'an 73:4 — "Recite the Qur'an in a slow and distinct manner."

147 Abū Dāwūd, *Sunan*, Witr, 20: an-Nasā'ī, *Sunan*, Iftitāḥ, 83; Ibn Māja, *Sunan*, Iqāma, 176; al-Bukhārī, *Ṣaḥīḥ*, Tawḥīd, 52.

148 Al-Bukhārī, *Ṣaḥīḥ*, Tawḥīd, 32, 52, Faḍā'il al-Qur'an, 19; Muslim, *Ṣaḥīḥ*, Musāfirīn, 232, 233, 234.

the house from the mosque]. She came late. The Prophet asked her, "What has prevented you [from returning earlier]?" She replied, "Messenger of God, I was listening to the Qur'an-reading of a man; I have never heard any voice sweeter than his." The Prophet (may God bless him and greet him!) stood up, [went to the mosque], and listened to his Qur'an-reading for a long time. On returning to the house he (may God bless him and greet him!) said, "This man is Sālim, a freed slave of Abū Ḥudhayfa.[149] Praise be to God Who has made a man like him in my community!" One night the Prophet (may God bless him and greet him!) also listened to the Qur'an-reading of 'Abd Allāh Ibn Mas'ūd, and with the Prophet were Abū Bakr and 'Umar (may God be pleased with them both!). They stood still for a long time [listening]. Then the Prophet [279] (may God bless him and greet him!) said, "One who wants to read the Qur'an as fresh as it was revealed should read it following the reading of Ibn Umm 'Abd."[150] The Prophet (may God bless him and greet him!) asked Ibn Mas'ūd, "Read the Qur'an to me." He replied, "Messenger of God, I should read it to you, and it is to you that it was revealed!" The Prophet (may God bless him and greet him!) said "I should like to hear it from others." Then Ibn Mas'ūd went on reading, and the eyes of the Messenger of God (may God bless him and greet him!) were shedding tears.[151] The Prophet (may God bless him and greet him!) listened to the Qur'an-reading of Abū Mūsā,[152] and remarked, "This man is bestowed with the sweet voice

149 Sālim, a freed slave of Abū Ḥudhayfa Ibn 'Utba Ibn Rabī'a, was one of those companions of the Prophet who migrated to Medina at an early stage, and who took part at the battle of Badr. The Prophet specified four of his companions from whom others should learn Qur'an-reading, and Sālim was one of these four. Abū Ḥudhayfa was also a companion of the Prophet. Both Sālim and Abū Ḥudhayfa together became martyrs at the battle of Yamāma during the caliphate of Abū Bakr. See Ibn 'Abd al-Barr, *op. cit.*, II, 68ff.; Ibn Ḥajar, *op. cit.*, II, 6ff.

150 Ibn Māja, *Sunan*, Muqaddama, 11; Ibn Ḥanbal, *Musnad*, I, 7, 26, 38, 445.

151 Al-Bukhārī, *Ṣaḥīḥ*, Faḍā'il aṣ-Ṣaḥāba, 25, Faḍā'il al-Qur'an, 33, 35; at-Tirmidhī, *Sunan*, Janā'iz, 14; an-Nasā'ī, *Sunan*, Janā'iz, 27. The eyes of the Prophet shed tears when Ibn Mas'ūd recited the verse (4:41), "How will it be when [on the Day of Judgement] We shall bring a witness from every people, and shall bring you [i.e. the Prophet] as a witness against these?"

152 Abū Mūsā 'Abd Allāh Ibn Qays al-Anṣārī (d. 42 or 44 A.H.), a companion of the Prophet, was an early Muslim. The Prophet appointed him the governor of part of the Yemen. 'Umar and 'Uthmān appointed him the governor of Basra and Kufa respectively. He was 'Alī's judge at Ṣiffīn. He was a great narrator of Traditions and an expert in legal matters. He was well known for his sweet voice at Qur'an-recitation.

of [the prophet] David."[153] This remark reached the ear of Abū Mūsā who then said, "Messenger of God, had I known that you were listening I would have adorned it fully."[154] Haytham,[155] the Qur'an-reader, saw the Prophet (may God bless him and greet him!) in a dream and then related, "He asked me [in the dream], 'Are you that Haytham who adorns the Qur'an with your voice?' I replied, 'Yes'. He prayed for me saying, 'May God grant you a good recompense!' " It is related in a Tradition: When several companions of the Messenger of God (may God bless him and greet him!) assembled, they used to order one of them to read a sura of the Qur'an. 'Umar used to request Abū Mūsā (may God be pleased with them both!), "Remind us of our Lord". So he used to read the Qur'an until about the middle of the time allowed for ritual prayer. Someone used to say, "The Commander of the Believers, ritual prayer, ritual prayer!" He replied, "Are we not already in prayer?," indicating to the words of God (great and mighty is He!), "The remembrance of God is the greatest" (ولذكر الله اكبر).[156] The Prophet (may God bless him and greet him!) said, "For one who listens to the recitation of a verse from the Book of God (great and mighty is He!), it will be a [means of] light on the Day of Resurrection,"[157] It is mentioned in a Tradition that for him [the reward of] ten good deeds will be recorded. Since the reward of listening to Qur'an-recitation is great, and since it is the reciter who is the cause of it, he will partake in the reward, except if the motive of his recitation is ostentation (*riyā'*) and affectation.[158]

See Ibn Ḥajar, *op. cit.*, II, 351f.; Ibn 'Abd al-Barr, *op. cit.*, II, 363ff.

153 For this meaning of the phrase *'mazāmīr āl Dāwūd'* see az-Zabīdī, *op. cit.*, IV, 499. For the sweet voice of the prophet David see aṭ-Ṭabarī, *Tārīkh al-Umam wa l-Mulūk*, Egypt, n.d., I, 248.

154 Al-Bukhārī, *Ṣaḥīḥ*, Faḍā'il al-Qur'an, 31; Muslim, *Ṣaḥīḥ*, Musāfirīn, 235, 236.

155 Al-Haytham Ibn Ḥumayd al-Ghassānī was very famous for Qur'an-recitation. He was a trustworthy (*thiqa*) Traditionist as well. See Ibn Qutayba, *op. cit.*, p. 533.

156 Qur'an 29:45.

157 Ibn Ḥanbal, *Musnad*, II, 341.

158 See *supra*, n. 143.

CHAPTER THREE

MENTAL TASKS IN QUR'AN-RECITATION

الذين اتيناهم الكتاب يتلونه حق تلاوته. اولئك يوءمنون به – قرآن ١٢١ : ٢

Those whom We have given the Book (Qur'an) recite it as it should be recited; they believe in it. — Qur'an 2 : 121

افلا يتدبرون القرأن ام على قلوب اقفالها؟ – قرأن ٢٤:٨٧

Do they not ponder over the Qur'an, or is it that their minds are locked up from within? — Qur'an 87 : 24

اقرءوا القرأن والتمسوا غرائبه

Read the Qur'an and seek to know its deep, strange meanings. — prophet Muḥammad

MENTAL TASKS IN QUR'AN-RECITATION ARE TEN IN NUMBER

The mental tasks in recitation of the Qur'an are [first] understanding the origin of the speech [i.e. the Qur'an], then magnification of it, then paying attention to it, then pondering over it, then understanding [its meanings], then getting rid of obstacles to this understanding, then specification [of all addresses of the Qur'an with oneself], then influencing the mind [with the theme of verses recited], then gradual rising [to the highest stage of recitation], and then the denial of one's own ability and power [independent of God].

[1]

The first mental task is understanding the magnification of the divine speech [i.e. the Qur'an] and its elevated nature, and the bounty of God (glorified and exalted is He!) and His kindness towards His creatures [i.e. men] in descending from the throne of His majesty to the level of their understanding.

The Qur'an-reader should consider how God showed kindness towards men in delivering to their understanding the meanings of His speech which is His eternal attribute existing with His essence.[159] [He should also consider] how that attribute is revealed

159 This is the Ash'arite view which is in sharp contrast with the well known

to them in the form of letters and sounds which are attributes of human beings, because man is unable to reach the stage of understanding the attributes of God (great and mighty is He!) except through his own attributes. If the inmost majesty of His speech were not concealed in the garment of letters, neither His throne nor [even] the subsoil would have remained fixed as a result of hearing His speech, and all that is between these two would have been reduced to nothing because of the greatness of His authority and the majesty of His light. If God (great and mighty is He!) had not strengthened Moses (may peace be upon him!) he would not have been able to hear His words in the way the mountain could not bear the beginnings of His manifestation so that it broke into bits.[160]

It is not possible to make the magnification of divine speech intelligible to men except through examples on the levels of their understanding. For this reason a certain gnostic (*'ārif*) explained the divine speech by saying, "Every letter of the words of God (great and mighty is He!) in the Preserved Tablet (*al-Lawḥ al-Maḥfūẓ*)[161] is greater than the mountain Qāf;[162] and if the angels (may peace be

heretical theory of the Mu'tazilites that the divine speech is created (*ḥādith*). In the *Jawāhir*, p. 19 al-Ghazālī strongly criticizes this theory.

160 This refers to the Qur'anic verse (7:143): "When Moses arrived at the Tryst at Our appointed time and his Lord spoke to him, he said, 'Lord, show Yourself to me that I may see You.' He replied, 'You can never see Me, but look towards the mountain; if it remains firm in its place you will soon see Me.' When his Lord manifested Himself on the mountain, He broke it into bits and Moses fell into a faint. When he recovered he exclaimed, 'Glory be to You! I turn wholly towards You, and I am the foremost among those who believe.' "

161 The Preserved Tablet is commonly understood to be in heaven. It contains the originals of all revealed Books including the Qur'an (Qur'an 13:39). Everything which God has decreed to bring into being from the beginning of creation to Doomsday is recorded in it (Qur'an 22:52). It is referred to sometimes as the Tablet, sometimes as a Clear Book, and sometimes as a Clear Imām. See az-Zamakhsharī, *op. cit.*, II, 363, 539; al-Ghazālī, *Iḥyā'*, IV, 504-505.

162 Qāf is the name of the mountain range surrounding the earth. Like the Hebrews and the Greeks in the period of Homer, Hesiod and the Ionian physicists, the ancient Arabs usually regarded the earth as a quite flat, circular disc. The mountain Qāf is separated from the disc of the earth by a region impassable to men. Another view connected with Greek and Iranian ideas regards the earth as immediately surrounded by a stinking, unnavigable body of water called al-Baḥr al-Muḥīṭ, or Uqiyānūs (Okeanos) which in whole or part is veiled in deep darkness and whose shores no one knows. The whole, earth and sea, is then held together by the mountain wall Qāf as by a ring. See M. Streck, "Ḳāf", *EI*, II, 614-615.

upon them!) join together to bear a single letter they will not be able to do so until Isrāfīl[163] (may peace be upon him!) who is the angel entrusted with the Preserved Tablet, comes to it and lifts it; and he becomes able to bear it by the permission of God (great and mighty is He!) and by His mercy, not by his own power and ability but God (great and mighty is He!) has bestowed upon him the power to do this and employed him in this task."

A certain wise man has very carefully explained the manner of God's kindness in delivering the meanings of His speech, despite its exalted nature, to man's understanding and His strengthening him despite his imperfect status. This wise man has set forth a parable which he told in full. This as follows: A wise man invited [280] a certain king to the Sharī'a (revealed law) of prophets (may peace be upon them!). The king questioned him concerning several matters [related to the oneness of God]. The wise man answered in such a way that the king was able to understand.[164] Then the king asked him, "Tell me, concerning that which the prophets bring [from God], when a claim is made [by them] that it is not the speech of a human being but the speech of God (great and mighty is He!), how can man understand it?" The wise man replied, "We have seen that when a man seeks to make some lower animals and birds understand what he wants them to do, such as to proceed, to delay, to come forth, and to turn back, and [when he] sees that the discriminating sense of these lower animals [and birds] falls short of understanding his speech which proceeds from the lights of his intellects and which has beauty, adornment and flowering of order — then he descends to the level of the discriminating sense of the lower animals and delivers his intentions to these animals through sounds made suitable to them, such as calling and whistling, and through sounds

163 Isrāfīl is the greatest of all angels. His greatness is brought to the mind by such expression as: While his feet are under the seventh earth, his head reaches up to the pillars of the throne of God. He is in charge of the Preserved Tablet. He is called the possessor of the trumpet, because since the start of creation he has continually been holding the trumpet to his mouth and will have been continually holding it in the same way until the Doomsday in order to be able to blow at once as soon as God gives the order for the blast. He will blow it twice. When the first sounding is given all that is in the heavens and all that is in the earth will be struck senseless, save only those whom God pleases. [After forty years] he will blow it again and they will immediately be standing up looking around (Qur'an 39:62), and then will move towards the field of resurrection for judgement.

164 يحتمله فهمه (BE: لا يحتمله فهمه).

near to their own sounds so that they may be able to understand him.[165]

"In like manner, human beings are unable to understand the speech of God (great and mighty is He!) to its inmost depth and to the perfection of its attributes. So it, in sounds which they (i.e. human beings) use among themselves and through which they have heard divine wisdom, has become like the sound of calling and whistling which the lower animals have heard from men. This did not prevent the meanings of divine wisdom, hidden in those attributes, from making the speech, i.e. sounds, noble because of the nobility of divine wisdom and magnified because of the magnification of it. The sounds have become [like] the body and the dwelling place for divine wisdom, and divine wisdom has become [like] the soul and spirit for the sounds. Just as human bodies are honoured and respected because they are the dwelling place for the soul,[166] so the sounds of divine speech are considered noble because of the divine wisdom that exists in them. The divine speech has an exalted status, a high grade, a subduing authority, and is an executor of judgement in respect of truth and falsehood. It is the just judge, the pleasing witness, and one which commands and prohibits. Falsehood has no power to stand up in front of divine speech filled with wisdom,[167] just as a shadow is unable to stand up in front of sun-rays. Human beings have no power to penetrate into the depth of divine wisdom, just as they have no power to penetrate with their eyes into the light of the sun itself. They, however, attain from the light of the sun itself only that which their eyes can bear and which enables them to seek information about their needs. Divine speech then is like a veiled king whose face is unknown [but] whose decree is carried out, like the sun which is mighty and obvious [but] the essence of which is hidden, and like shining stars by which one, although not acquainted with their course, goes in the right way. It is, then, the key to precious treasures, a drink of life from which, if anyone drinks, he does not die, and a medicine from which, if

165 Cf. *Qūt,* I, 101.

166 In Islam the soul is the real man while the body is only its necessary vehicle or instrument. Through this instrument the soul achieves perfection and provision for its eternal life in the Hereafter. For a discussion on this see Quasem, *Ethics,* pp. 44-48, 72-74.

167 Cf. Qur'an 41:42.

anyone takes a dose, he does not fall ill." [168]

The words of the wise man are a fragment of what is needed for one to understand the meaning of divine speech. More than this is not appropriate to the science of practical religion (*'ilm al-mu'āmala*). So one should be content with this.

[2]

The second mental task is magnification of the Speaker [in the Qur'an].

At the start of Qur'an-recitation the reciter should bring to his mind magnification of the One Who speaks [in the Qur'an, i.e. God], and should realize that what he is reading is not the speech of a human being, and that in the recitation of the speech of God (great and mighty is He!) there is an extreme danger, because God (exalted is He!) said, "Only those who are clean can touch it" (لا يمسه الا المطهرون).[169] Just as the external side of the leather of *muṣḥaf* and its pages are protected against the external skin of a person who touches it except when he is pure [both physically and ritually], so also its internal meaning is veiled, by the authority of its greatness and might, from the internal aspect of the reciter's mind, except when it is pure from all defilement and is illuminated by the light of magnification and reverence. Just as every hand is not fit for touching the leather of *muṣḥaf*, so also every tongue is not fit to recite its letters, nor every mind fit to understand its meanings. It is due to such magnification that 'Ikrima Ibn Abī Jahal,[170] when he opened the *muṣḥaf* for reading, used to fall faint saying, "This is the speech of my Lord, this is the speech of my Lord!" Thus the magnification of the speech [i.e. the Qur'an] is [in effect] the magnification of the Speaker [i.e. God].

Magnification of the Speaker [in the Qur'an, i.e. God] will never come to [the mind of] the Qur'an-reciter unless he reflects on His

[168] Al-Ghazālī has taken this parable from al-Makkī's *Qūt*, I, 101-102.

[169] Qur'an 56:79.

[170] 'Ikrima Ibn Abī Jahal (d. 15. A.H./636 A.D.) was a companion of the Prophet. He embraced Islam in 8 A.H. Just as before conversion he took a leading part against Islam so also after conversion he showed great zeal for it, and both during and after the lifetime of the Prophet rendered remarkable services to the cause of Islam. He died as a martyr (*shahīd*) in the fighting in Syria. See Ibn, 'Abd al-Barr, *op. cit.*, III, 148-51.

attributes, His majesty and His works. Thus when the idea of the throne [of God], of the heavens, of the earth, and of all that is between these two, such as the jinn,[171] man, other moving creatures, and trees, comes to his mind, and he knows with certainty [a] that the creator of all of these, who has power over them and who sustains them, is the One Who has no partner, and [b] that all, being within the grip of His power, move between His bounty and mercy and between His revenge and assault — if He bestows favour upon them this is through His bounty and if He punishes them this is by His justice[172] —, and [c] that He is the One Who says, "These [i.e. the people on the right] will go to Paradise and I do not hesitate to do this, and these [i.e. the people on the left] will go to Hell and I do not hesitate to do this", and this is the end of magnification and elevation — then reflection on these and other similar things will bring to the mind of the Qur'an-reader the magnification of the Speaker [in the Qur'an, i.e. God] first and then the magnification of the speech [i.e. the Qur'an].

[3]

The third mental task is to pay attention and abandon the inner utterances of the soul (*ḥadīth an-nafs*).

In the explanation of [the verse], "Yaḥyā,[173] hold fast the Book" (يا يحيى، خذ الكتاب بقوة),[174] it is said that "hold fast" means to read with serious endeavour and diligence. Holding the Book with serious endeavour consists in one's being isolated with it when reading it and turning all one's attention to it and away from other things. A certain gnostic was asked, "When you read the Qur'an does your soul make inner utterances concerning any matter?" He replied, "Is there anything preferable to the Qur'an so that my soul

171 See *supra*, n. 11.

172 This is an article of faith (*'aqīda*) according to the People of the Sunna and the Community (*Ahl as-Sunna wa l-Jamā'a*). For an explanation of it see al-Ghazālī, *Iḥyā'*, I, 91.

173 Yaḥyā Ibn Zakariyya (John the Baptist) was a prophet mentioned in the Qur'an along with Jesus, Elijah (Ilyās) and a few other prophets (Qur'an 3:39, 6:85, 19:7, 19:12, 21:90). The Book mentioned in the Qur'anic verse 19:12 is the Torah, the Pentateuch. Yaḥyā did not receive a special revelation from God; his mission was only to confirm the word of God; God gave him understanding of the Torah. See B. Carra de Vaux, "Yaḥyā," *SEI*, p. 640.

174 Qur'an 19:12.

may make inner utterances concerning it?" A certain righteous father (*ba'ḍ as-salaf*), if he read a verse without giving the full attention of his mind to it, used to read it a second time.

This attribute [i.e. attention of the mind to the verses recited] is generated from the preceding attribute which is magnification [of the Speaker], because a person who magnifies the speech [of God] which he is reciting draws a good omen from it, has warm relations with it and is not inattentive to it. In the Qur'an is present that with which the soul can have warm relations if the reciter is fit for it. How can it seek an intimate connection with the thought of anything other than the Qur'an, seeing that the reciter is in a pleasant place [175] and a place relieved of cares [281], and one who is relieved of cares in a pleasant place [176] does not think of another place? It is said that in the Qur'an are to be found fields, gardens, closets, brides, brocades, meadows, and khans. All *mīms* are the fields of the Qur'an; all *rā's* are the gradens; all *hā's* are its closets; all suras starting with the glorification of God are its brides, all suras starting with the letters *ḥā mīm* are its brocades, all the suras in which laws, stories, etc. are expounded are its meadows, and all other parts of it are its khans. When the Qur'an-reader enters into the fields of the Qur'an, plucks different types of fruits from its gardens, enters into its closets, views the brides, wears the brocades, is relieved of cares, and dwells in the khans, then all these absorb him wholly and keep him from things other than these; consequently his mind cannot be inattentive, nor can his thought be separated.

[4]

The fourth mental task is pondering [over the verse recited].[177] This is more than attention of the mind, because sometimes [it so happens that] a man who is reading the Qur'an is not thinking about anything else but is confining himself to listening to it, whereas he is not pondering over it.

The purpose of reading the Qur'an is to ponder over it. For this reason it is sunna to read the Qur'an in a slow and distinct manner (*tartīl*).[178] Reading the Qur'an in this manner outwardly is sunna in

175 منتزه (BE: متنزه). 176 المنتزهات (BE: المتنزهات).

177 Cf. Qur'an 47:24 — "Do they not ponder over the Qur'an or is it that their minds are locked up from within?"

178 Cf. Qur'an 73:4 — "Recite the Qur'an in a slow and distinct manner."

order that pondering over it inwardly may be strengthened. 'Alī Ibn Abī Ṭālib (may God be pleased with him!) said, "There is no good in a devotional act which is not understood [by its agent], nor in Qur'an-reading which is not pondered over."

Since pondering over verses is only strengthened by repetition the reciter should repeat them, except when he is performing ritual prayer following an *imām*.[179] [In this case] if he is still engaged in pondering on a verse [recited by the *imām*] whereas the *imām* has passed on to another verse, he will be a sinner. He is like a man whose astonishment at a sentence uttered by a person whispering to him keeps him from understanding the remaining part of what that person says. Likewise [the follower will be a sinner] if he is engaged in the glorification of God in the bowing (*tasbīḥ ar-rukū'*)[180] but is still thinking on a verse [read by his *imām* or by himself]. This is an evil suggestion [given by Satan]. It is related from 'Āmir Ibn 'Abd Qays[181] that he said, "Evil suggestions overwhelm me in ritual prayer." He was asked "Concerning wordly matters?" He replied, "I would prefer to be pierced by spear-heads to that. But my mind is engaged in thought about standing in front of God (great and mighty is He!) [on the Day of Judgement],[182] and about how I shall depart from there [being one of those received by God or those rejected]." He considered this an evil suggestion [despite its being a religious thought]. It was really an evil suggestion, because it kept him from understanding the ritual prayer in which he was engaged. Satan is only able to deceive a man like him by engaging him in an important religious thought but thereby preventing him from that which is the best. When the words of 'Āmir were mentioned to al-Ḥasan he said, "If you are truthful in relating his words, God has not ordered that for us."

It is related that [one night] the Prophet (may God bless him and

179 See *supra*, n. 123.

180 The formula of this glorification is: سبحان ربى العظيم (glorified is my Lord, the great!).

181 'Āmir Ibn 'Abd Qays, al-'Anbārī, a Follower, was an ascetic and Traditionist of Basra. He died in Damascus during the caliphate of Mu'awiya. In the eyes of posterity he is not only an eloquent man whose sayings have been preserved, but ṣūfism, which includes him among the eight principal ascetics among the Followers, still recognizes him as a forerunner and attributes to him a number of miracles. See al-Munāwī, *op. cit.*, I, 128f.

182 This refers to the Qur'anic verse 79:40-41.

greet him!) read "In the name of God, Most Gracious, Ever Merciful"(بسم الله الرحمن الرحيم)[183] and repeated it twenty times. Certainly he (may God bless him and greet him!) repeated it in order to ponder over its meanings. It is related from Abū Dharr that he said, "One night the Messenger of God (may God bless him and greet him!) kept vigil at night along with us. He kept vigil repeating a single verse which is, 'If You punish them [i.e. people] surely they are your servants, and if You forgive them surely You are the Mighty, the Wise' (ان تعذبهم فانهم عبادك، وان تغفرلهم فانك غفور الرحيم).[184] "[185]

Tamīm ad-Dārī[186] kept vigil one night with this verse: "Do those who commit evil deeds imagine that We shall make them as those who believe and do good deeds in life and in death? How evil is that which they judge!" (ام حسب الذين اجتراحوا السيئات الاية).[187] Sa'īd Ibn Jubayr[188] kept vigil one night repeatedly reciting the verse, "[A command will go forth on the Day of Judgement:] Separate Yourselves [from the righteous] this day, O you guilty ones" (وامتازوا اليوم، ايها المجرمون).[189] A certain righteous father said, "I start reading a sura and then some [wonderful meanings] which I view in it keeps me from completing it until the dawn appears." A certain pious man used to say, "I do not reckon that there is any reward for reading a verse which I do not understand and to which my mind does not give attention [when I read it]." It is related from Abū Sulaymān ad-Dārānī that he said, "I certainly recite a verse and then remain with it thinking for four or five nights. Unless I cut off my thinking on it I do not pass on to another verse." It is related from a certain righteous father that he remained in the Sura of Hūd[190] for six months, continuously repeating it and pondering over it. A certain gnostic said, "I completed the reading of the entire Qur'an

183 Qur'an 1:1. 184 Qur'an 5:118.

185 An-Nasā'ī, *Sunan*, Iftitāḥ, 69; Ibn Māja, *Sunan*, Iqāma, 179.

186 Tamīm ad-Dārī was a great companion of the Prophet. He led an ascetic life and was regular in keeping vigil at night. He died in Syria. See al-Munāwī, *op. cit.*, I, 50; Ibn Ḥajar, *op. cit.*, I, 186; Ibn 'Abd al-Barr, *op. cit.*, I, 186f.

187 Qur'an 45:21.

188 Sa'īd Ibn Jubayr (d. 95 A.H.), one of the leading Followers, was noted for his knowledge of Qur'anic exegesis, Tradition and jurisprudence, and for his devotion and piety. He transmitted Traditions from a number of great companions of the Prophet. He was killed by Ḥajjāj Ibn Yūsuf. See an-Nawawī, *op. cit.*, I, 216f.

189 Qur'an 36:59.

190 This is the eleventh sura of the Qur'an consisting of one hundred and twenty-three verses. The Prophet said that this sura made his hair white, because in

[sometimes] on every Friday, [sometimes] every month, and [sometimes] every year. For the last thirty years I have been trying to complete the reading of the entire Qur'an [with deep understanding of its meanings] but have not yet been able to do so." These differences are according to different depths of his pondering over the Qur'an and of his discovery of its meanings. This gnostic also used to say, "I have put myself in the place of servants in the matter of devotion. I perform acts of devotion on four different courses — by the day, by the week (Friday), by the month and by the year."

[5]

The fifth mental task is understanding [the meaning of verses recited].

This is to seek, from [the meaning of] every verse [recited], explanations which befit it, since the Qur'an encompasses the discussion of the attributes of God (great and mighty is He!), discussion of His works, the discussion of the circumstances of prophets (may peace be upon them!), the discussion of the circumstances of those who considered them false and of how they were destroyed, the description of God's commandments and threats, and the description of Paradise and Hell.[191]

As for the attributes of God (great and mighty is He!), they are put, for example, in His (exalted is He!) words, "Like Him there is nothing. He is All-hearing, All-seeing" (ليس كمثله شيىء وهوالسميع البصير);[192] and in His (exalted is He!) words, "He [i.e. God] is the Sovereign, the Most Holy, the Source of Peace, the Bestower of Security, the Protector, the Mighty, the Subduer, the Exalted" (الملك القدوس السلام الموءمن المهمين العزيز الجبار المتكبر).[193] The Qur'an-reader should reflect on the meanings of these names and attributes of God so that deep connotations may be disclosed to him. Underneath them are hidden meanings [282] which can only be disclosed to those especially favoured [by God] to understand them. It is to this that 'Alī (may God be pleased with him!) indicated by his

this sura God commanded him, "Continue to stand upright, as you have been commanded, along with those who have turned wholly to God with you; do not exceed the bounds; surely God sees very well all that you do" (11:12). This uprightness is not an easy matter.

191 All this is discussed in some detail in al-Ghazālī's *Jawāhir*, pp. 9-17.

192 Qur'an 42:11.

193 Qur'an 59:23.

words, "The Messenger of God (may God bless him and greet him!) did not hide from me anything which he concealed from people, except that God (great and mighty is He!) bestows upon a man understanding of His Book."[194] The Qur'an-reader should be greedy in seeking this understanding. Ibn Mas'ūd (may God be pleased with him!) said, "One who wants to acquire [the core principles of] the knowledge of the ancients and the moderns should deeply study the Qur'an". The greatest of all forms of knowledge of the Qur'an is under the names of God (great and mighty is He!) and His attributes; most people could only know about them certain matters suitable to their understanding and could not obtain knowledge of their depths.

As for the works of God (exalted is He!), they are discussed, for example, in His discussion of the creation of the heavens, the earth, and other things [such as rivers and mountains]. The Qur'an-reciter should understand from them the attributes of God (great and mighty is He!), since the existence of a work proves the existence of its Agent, and the greatness of the former proves the greatness of the latter. So he should view in the act the Agent and not the act. One who knows the True One sees Him in everything since everything originates from Him, returns to Him, subsists by Him and belongs to Him. Thus He is the all in reality. He who does not see Him in everything which he sees, is as if he does not know Him. One who knows Him knows that 'everything save God is false'[195] and that 'everything will perish except Himself (lit. His face).'[196] The meaning of this is not that everything will be falsehood in a second condition; rather it is falsehood now if its essence is

194 An-Nasā'ī, *Sunan*, Qasāma, 13; al-Bukhārī, *Ṣaḥīḥ*, Diyyāt, 24, 31; Ibn Ḥanbal, *Musnad*, I, 79.

195 This *expression* seems to have been derived from the well known *Dīwān* of Labīd Ibn Rabī'a (d. 40, 41 or 42 A.H.), an Arab poet of the pagan period who lived into the days of Islam and who became a companion of the Prophet in 9 A.H. (an-Nawawī, *op. cit.*, II, 70f.; Ibn Ḥajar, *op. cit.*, III, 307-309; Ibn 'Abd al-Barr, *op. cit.*, III, 306-310. The verse of the *Dīwān* which seems to have influenced al-Ghazālī's *expression* is: الا كل شيىء ماخلا الله باطل – وكل نعيم لامحالة زائل

The Prophet called this verse: "The truest words which any poet has ever spoken." See al-Bukhārā, *Ṣaḥīḥ*, Adab, 90, Manāqib al-Anṣār, 26; Muslim, *Ṣaḥīḥ*, Shi'r, 3-6; Ibn Māja, *Sunan*, Adab, 41. As-Sarrāj has also cited this verse of Labīd in his *Luma'*, p. 110.

196 Qur'an 28:88.

considered in respect of itself, but is not falsehood if its existence is considered in respect of the fact that it exists through God (great and mighty is He!) and His power. So it has existence by way of following [God] and is sheer falsehood by way of independence [from God]. This is one of the principles of knowledge achieved through mystical intuition.

For this reason the Qur'an-reader — when he reads the words of God (great and mighty is He!) which ask , "Have you considered that which you sow?"(افرأيتم ما تحرثون),[197] "Have you reflected on the sperm-drop that you emit?"(افرأيتم ما تمنون),[198] "Have you reflected on the water that you drink?"(افرأيتم الماء الذى تشربون),[199] "Have you reflected on the fire that you kindle?"(افرأيتم النار التى تورون)[200] — should not confine his thoughts to water, fire, seeds, and sperm-drops. Rather he should reflect on the sperm-drop and know first that it is a small quantity of water-like substance the parts of which resemble one another. Then he should consider how it is [gradually] divided into flesh, bones, nerves and veins and how its limbs take different features — head, hands, legs, liver, heart, and others. Then he should consider those noble attributes that make themselves manifest in it — hearing, seeing, thinking and others. Then he should consider the condemnable attributes that appear in it — anger, desire, pride, ignorance, lying and quarrelling, as God (exalted is He!) said, "Has not man considered that We have created him from a mere sperm-drop? Then he clearly disputes [the existence of his Creator]!"(اولم يرالانسان انا خلقناه من نطفة؟ فاذا هو خصيم مبين!)[201] Then the Qur'an-reader will reflect on these wonders so that he may ascend from them to a higher wonder of these wonders which is the attribute from which these wonders have proceeded. He will persistently be considering the making so that he will see the Maker.

As for the circumstances of the prophets (may peace be upon them!), when the Qur'an-reader hears how they[202] were considered false, beaten, and some of them were [even] killed he should understand from this God's (great and mighty is He!) attribute of independence from His messengers and from those to whom they were sent, and that if He destroyed all of them this will not affect anything in His kingdom. When he hears of God's help to the

197 Qur'an 56:63.
198 Qur'an 56:58.
199 Qur'an 56:68.
200 Qur'an 56:71.
201 Qur'an 36:77.
202 انهم , which is omitted in BE.

Messengers in the end, he should understand the power of God (great and mighty is He!) and His will to further the truth.

As for the circumstances of the deniers of God, e.g. the people of 'Ād[203] and the people of Thamūd,[204] and the evil that happened to them, the Qur'an-reader's understanding of these should result in a feeling of fear of God's assault and His revenge; and he should give special consideration to his [own] portion of these and remember that if he is inattentive [to his religious duties] and ill-mannered and is deceived by the delay of punishment which is accorded to him, divine revenge may overtake him and the sentence [of punishment] may be executed.

Likewise, when the Qur'an-reader hears the descriptions of Paradise and Hell and all other things in the Qur'an, e.g. promises and threats, hope and fear, he should try to understand the meanings proper to each case. It is not possible to enquire about that which will be understood from this description,[205] for that has no end, but everyone gets from it[206] that measure of valid understanding which is vouchsafed to him. 'There is nothing green nor dry but is is recordedin a ClearBook' (فلا رطب ولا يابس الا فى كتاب مبين).[207] 'Tell [people]: If the ocean became ink for [transcribing] the words of my Lord, surely the ocean would be exhausted before the words of my lord came to an end, even though We augmented it with the like of it' (قل لو كان البحر مدادا لكلمات ربى، لنفد البحر قبل ان تنفد كلمات ربى، ولو جئنا بمثله مددا).[208] It is for this reason that 'Ali (may God be pleased with him!) said, "If I will I can load seventy camels with the exegesis of the Sura of the Opening of the Book." The purpose of what we have discussed above is only to indicate the method of understanding [Qur'anic verses] so that the door of it may be opened to the reciter.

203 'Ād is an ancient tribe mentioned in the Qur'an as well as in pre-Islamic poetry. It was a mighty nation that lived immediately after the time of the prophet Noah, and became haughty on account of its great prosperity. It disobeyed the prophet Hūd who was one of its people, and on account of this, they were, with the exception of Hūd and a few pious men, swept away by a violent storm. See Qur'an 7:65, 74, 9:70, 11:50, 59, 60, 14:9, *passim*.

204 Thamūd is the name of one of those old Arabian peoples which had disappeared some time before the advent of Islam. The prophet Ṣāliḥ was sent to guide this people along the right path. The whole people was destroyed when it disobeyed him. See Qur'an 7:73, 9:70, 11:61, 68, 95, 14:9, *passim*.

205 منه (ZB: منها). 206 منه is omitted in BE. 207 Qur'an 6:59.

208 Qur'an 18:109.

To fathom it is not the coveted thing in this respect. One who has no understanding of what is in the Qur'an, even though this understanding is of the smallest degree, is included in the words of God (exalted is He!), "Some of them appear to listen to you [i.e. Muḥammad], but when they [283] go forth from your presence they ask those who have been given knowledge: What has he been talking about just now? These are they whose minds God has sealed up" (ومنهم من يستمع اليك، حتى اذا خرجوا من عندك، قالوا للذين اوتوا العلم: ماذا قال انفا؟ أولئك الذين طبع الله على قلوبهم).[209] That by which God sealed up [their minds] consists in the obstacles which we shall soon discuss in connection with the obstacles of understanding [the Qur'an]. It is said [by a gnostic], "A novice cannot be a [perfect] novice until he finds in the Qur'an everything that he wants and until he can distinguish between decreasing and increasing benefits [from reading it] and feels sufficient with his Master as opposed to people."

[6]

The sixth mental task is getting rid of the obstacles to the understanding of the Qur'an.

Most people are hindered from understanding the meanings of the Qur'an for reasons and veils let down on their minds by Satan so that the wonders of the secrets of the Qur'an have become obscure to them. The Prophet (may God bless him and greet him!) said, "Had it not been the case that Satans hover round about the minds of the sons of Adam, they would have been able to look at the invisible world (*malakūt*)." The meanings of the Qur'an are among the sum-total of the invisible world. Everything which is beyond the senses and which can only be apprehended by the light of spiritual insight (*nūr al-baṣīra*) belongs to the invisible world.

The veils obstructing the understanding of the Qur'an are four in number. The first is the direction of all care to the exact pronunciation of the letters, by producing them from their right places [in the mouth and tongue]. This is done by a Satan entrusted with Qur'an-readers in order to turn them away from understanding the meanings of the words of God (great and mighty is He!). This Satan always induces them to echo the letters [of the divine speech], making them imagine that they have not come out from the right places. When the thought of a Qur'an-reader is thus confined to

209 Qur'an 47:16.

right places for pronouncing the letters of the Qur'an how can its meanings be fully clear to him? The greatest laughing-stock of Satan is one who obeys him in a deception like this.

The second veil is the Qur'an-reader's being a purely dogmatic follower (*muqallid*) of a school of thought (*madhhab*) which is derived from an authority, and on which he has remained very firm with a strong mental zeal, by merely following what he has heard, without arriving at it by spiritual insight and mystical vision (*mushāhada*). This is a person whose belief has shackled him from going beyond it. So it is not possible that any idea other than that in which he has believed should come to his mind. Thus his consideration is limited to what he has heard. If a distant flash of lightning [of knowledge] is seen and one of the meanings [of a Qur'anic verse] which is opposite to the meaning he heard [from an authority] appears to him, then the Satan of purely following a school of thought dogmatically attacks him severely, saying, "How can this [new] meaning come to your mind, seeing that it is contradictory to the meaning in which your forefathers believed?" So he considers the new meaning as a deception from Satan, and he remains at a distance from it and guards himself against the like of it.

For a reason similar to this the ṣūfīs have said that knowledge (*'ilm*) is a veil [between man and God], and by this knowledge they have meant those beliefs (*'aqā'id*) which most people have been firmly holding either by dogmatically following an authority or by mere reliance on casuistic sentences written by zealots of schools of thought and delivered to them. As for the real knowledge which is the uncovering of the actual condition of the thing known and which is a vision by the light of spiritual insight, how can it be a veil, seeing that it is the ultimate object of desire?

Pure dogmatic following of an authority (*taqlīd*) is sometimes false [in itself] and is, therefore, an obstacle to the understanding of the meaning [of the Qur'an]. An example of this is a man who has a [purely dogmatic] belief that God's *istiwā'* on the throne[210] means His being settled on it physically. Then in the case of [the divine name] 'the Holy One' (*al-Quddūs*),[211] for example, there comes to his mind the meaning that He is pure from all that is ascribable to His creation; but that purely dogmatic belief of his does not make it possible for this meaning to be firmly implanted in his mind. Had it

210 Qur'an 7:54, 10:3, 13:2, 20:5, 25:59, 33:4, 57:4.

211 Qur'an 59:23, 62:1.

become strengthened in his mind it would have led to a second meaning and a third, which would be inter-connected. But he hastens to drive this meaning away from his mind, because it contradicts his false belief which is held purely dogmatically.

Sometimes purely dogmatic following of an authority is true [in itself], but it too becomes an obstacle to understanding [the meanings of the Qur'an] and to the unveiling of them. The truth in which man is obliged to believe has stages and grades, and it has an external beginning and an internal end. Concentration of man's nature on the external aspect prevents him from reaching the internal end. [This constitutes a veil], as we have discussed in connection with the distinction between the external and internal knowledge made in *The Book of the Articles of Faith.*[212]

The third veil is man's insistence upon sin, or his being characterized by pride, or his being, in general, afflicted with worldly passion which he follows. These cause the darkness of the soul and its rust,[213] and are comparable to dirt accumulating upon a mirror. So they prevent the truth from reflecting upon the soul. They constitute the greatest of all veils of the soul, and it is by them that most people are veiled [from the meanings of the Qur'an]. When worldly desires greatly accumulate [in the soul] the meanings of divine speech are greatly veiled. When [worldly] burdens on the soul are made light, reflection on its meaning becomes near. Thus the soul is like a mirror, desires are like rust, the meanings of the Qur'an are like forms which are visible in a mirror, and training the soul by removing [worldly] desires is like polishing of the mirror.

For this reason the Prophet (may God bless him and greet him!) said, "If my community considers gold and silver coins [i.e. wealth] as something great, the awe of Islam will be pulled away from it [by God]. If it abandons the imperatives of goodness and the prohibition of evil it will be deprived of the blessings of revelation." — Fuḍayl commented, "That is, they will be deprived of the understanding of the Qur'an." God (great and mighty is He!) has made 'turning to Him in repentance' (*ināba*) a stipulation for the understanding of the Qur'an and for the receipt of admonition. Thus He (exalted is He!) said, "... a matter for contemplation and a source of admoni-

212 This is the second 'book' of the *Iḥyā'* consisting of thirty-six large pages (89-125).

213 صدئه (ZE: صداه).

tion for every servant that turns to Us" (تبصرة وذكرى لكل عبد منيب).[214] God (great and mighty is He!) also said, "None pays heed save he who turns to God" (وما يتذكر الا من ينيب).[215] God (exalted is He!) further said, "It is only those gifted with understanding who take heed" (انما يتذكر اولوا الالباب).[216] The man who has preferred the deception of this world to the delight of the Hereafter, [284] is not among those gifted with understanding, and this is why deep meanings of the Book are not revealed to him.

The fourth veil is present when a man has read the outward exegesis of the Qur'an and has formed the belief that Qur'anic sentences have only those meanings which have come down by tradition from Ibn 'Abbās, Mujāhid, and other exegetes [from the leading Followers (*tabi'ūn*), that meanings going beyond them are interpretations of the Qur'an by personal opinion (*tafsīr bi-r-ra'y*), and that 'he who has explained the Qur'an by his personal opinion has taken his place in Hell.'[217] This too is one of the great veils [which prevent the mind from understanding the meaning of the Qur'an]. We shall soon discuss the meaning of explanation of the Qur'an by personal opinion, in the fourth chapter [of this book]. We shall also argue there the views [a] that this belief contradicts[218] the words of 'Alī (may God be pleased with him!), "Except that God bestows understanding of the Qur'an upon a man,"[219] and [b] that if the correct meaning of the Qur'an were only that which has come down by tradition [from the leading exegetes], people would not have disagreed on it.

[7]

The seventh mental task is to render [the teachings of the Qur'an] specific. This means that the Qur'an-reader will suppose that every part of the Qur'an is intended for him. If he hears any command or

214 Qur'an 50:8. This verse in its full form runs thus: "We have spread out the earth, and placed therein firm mountains; and We have caused to grow therein all kinds of beautiful species in pairs; a matter for contemplation and a source of admonition for every servant that turns to Us."

215 Qur'an 4:13. This verse in its complete form is: "It is He Who shows you His signs, and sends down provision for you from heaven, but none pays heed save he who turns to God."

216 Qur'an 13:19. 217 At-Tirmidhī, *Sunan*, Tafsīr, 1.

218 يناقض (BE: الايناقض).

219 See *supra*, n. 194

prohibition [contained in a Qur'anic verse] he will suppose that he is the man commanded or will suppose that he is the man to whom the prohibition applies. If he hears any promise of reward or any threat of punishment, he will make the same assumption. If he hears stories of the ancients and the prophets he will know that they are not intended for chatting in the evening [by narrating them]; what is intended is that they should be considered; from their manifold descriptions should be derived the lesson which is needed. The narration of every story in the Qur'an is only intended to provide some benefit to the Prophet (may God bless him and greet him!) and to his community. This is why God (exalted is He!) referred to it as "that whereby We make your mind firm"(ما نثبت به فوادك).[220] The Qur'an-reader should suppose that God has made his mind firm by narrating in it[221] the stories of prophets, their patience while suffering [due to the actions of their people], and their firmness in religion while waiting for help from God (exalted is He!). How can he not suppose this, seeing that the Qur'an was revealed to the Messenger of God not only for him especially, but a spiritual cure, a guidance, a mercy,[222] and a light for all the worlds?

For this reason God (exalted is He!) commanded all to be grateful [to Him] for His favour in sending down the Book. Thus He (great and mighty is He!) commanded, "Keep in your mind the favour that God has bestowed upon you and that which He has sent down to you of the Book and wisdom, through which He exhorts you" (واذكروا نعمة الله عليكم وما أنزل عليكم من الكتاب والحكمة. يعظكم به).[223] God (great and mighty is He!) also said, "We have sent down to you a Book which contains admonitions for you; will you not then understand?" (ولقد انزلنا اليكم كتابا فيه ذكركم. افلا تعقلون؟)[224] We have sent down this Reminder [i.e. the Qur'an] to you that you may expound to the people [Our commandments] which have been sent down to them [through you]" (وانزلنا اليك الذكر لتبين للناس مانزل اليهم).[225] "Thus does God set forth to people their true conditions" (كذلك يضرب الله للناس امثالهم)[226] "Follow the highest of the commandments that have been sent down to you from your Lord" (واتبعوا احسن ما انزل اليكم من ربكم).[227] "These teachings are manifest proofs for people, and a guidance and a mercy for a people who have sure faith" (هذا بصائر

220 Qur'an 11:120. 221 فيه (BE: عليه). 222 Cf. Qur'an 17:82.
223 Qur'an 2:231. 224 Qur'an 21:10. 225 Qur'an 16:44. 226 Qur'an 47:3.
227 Qur'an 39:55.

(للناس وهدى ورحمة لقوم يوقنون).[228] "This Qur'an is an exposition for the people, a guidance and admonition for the God-fearing" (هذا بيان للناس وهدى وموعظة للمتقين).[229]

Since God's message is intended for all people, it is intended for individuals as well. Thus this Qur'an-reader, an individual, is intended. He has nothing to do with other people. Thus he should suppose that he is the one [for whom the message is] intended. God (exalted is He!) said, "[Tell people:] This Qur'an is revealed to me so that through it I may warn you and whomever it reaches" (واوحى الى هذا القرأن لانذركم به ومن بلغ).[230] Muḥammad Ibn al-Qurẓī said, "One whom the Qur'an reaches is as if spoken to by God."

If the Qur'an-reader supposes that every part of the Qur'an is intended for him he will not take up [mere] study of it as his duty;[231] rather he will read it just as a slave reads the writing of his master who has written to him so that he may think on it and act according to it. For this reason a certain religious scholar said, "This Qur'an consists of treatises which have come to us from our Lord (great and mighty is He!) bearing His covenants. We ponder over them in ritual prayers, busy ourselves with them in quiet places and execute them in acts of obedience to God and in following the Sunna of the Prophet." Mālik Ibn Dīnār[232] used to say, "The Qur'an is not planted in your minds, O people concerned with it. Surely it is that which should cause the flowering of the believer in spring just as rain is [that which causes] the flowering of the earth in spring" Qatada[233] said, "No one sits in the company of the Qur'an without standing up, having been harmed or benefited by it." God (exalted is He!) said,[234] "That (i.e. the Qur'an) is a [spiritual] cure and a mercy for the believers; but it only impels the wrongdoers into great ruin" (هو شفاء ورحمة للموءمنين، ولا يزيد الظالمين الا خسارا).[235]

[8]

228 Qur'an 45:20. 229 Qur'an 3:138. 230 Qur'an 6:19.

231 To take up mere study of the Qur'an as a duty is also condemned in al-Ghazālī's *Jawāhir*, pp. 8f.

232 Mālik Ibn Dīnār (d. 181 A.H.), a Follower, was a leading ascetic of Basra. He emphasized love of God and hope of divine mercy. See al-Munāwī, *op. cit.*, I, 154-57.

233 Qatāda Ibn Di'āma (d. 117 or 118 A.H.), a Follower, was an exegete, jurist and trustworthy Traditionist. He was also a scholar of Arab poetry. See an-Nawawī, *op. cit.*, II 57f.; adh-Dhahabī, *Tādhkira al-Ḥuffāẓ*, Hyderabad, India, 1333-34, I, 121-24.

234 قال الله تعالى (BE: قال تعالى).

235 Qur'an 17:34.

The eighth mental task is to feel the Qur'an. This means that the mind of the Qur'an-reader will be affected by different feelings according to the different verses recited. Thus in accordance with what his mind understands, he will be in a state of grief, fear, hope, and so on.

Whenever the Qur'an-reader's knowledge [of the meaning of verses recited] is perfect his fear will be the most predominant of all the states of the soul. The quality of making the mind straitened and sorrowful predominates Qur'anic verses. Thus the mention of divine forgiveness and divine mercy is always seen to be accompanied by stipulations which the reader falls short of attaining. An example of this is the words of God, "Verily I am Most Forgiving" (وانى لغفار).[236] Then God made this to be followed by four stipulations: "towards him who repents, believes, does good deeds, and then is rightly guided" (لمن تاب وامن وعمل صالحا ثم اهتدى)[237] Another example is the speech of God (exalted is He!), "I swear by time, surely man suffers continuous loss, except those who believe, do good deeds, exhort one another to hold fast to the truth, and exhort one another to patience" (والعصر ان الانسان لفى خسر الا الذين امنو وعملوا الصالحات، وتواصوا بالحق وتواصوا بالصبر).[238] Here God has mentioned four stipulations but when He is content [with the mention of a single stipulation] He has pointed out a stipulation which covers all [the stipulations mentioned above]. Thus He (exalted is He!) said, "Surely the mercy of God is near to those who carry out their duty to the utmost" (ان رحمة الله قريب من المحسنين).[239] The stipulation of carrying out one's duty to the utmost includes all [stipulations]. Such method as this will be found by one who examines the Qur'an from its beginning to the end. The man who understands this in his Qur'an-recitation will be in a mental state of fear and grief. For this reason al-Ḥasan said, "I swear by God, a man who, in the morning, recites the Qur'an believing in it, will find that his grief increases and his joy decreases, his weeping increases and his laughter decreases, and his weariness and work increase while his rest and relaxation decrease." Wuhayb Ibn al-Ward said, "We have considered Traditions and sermons but have not found anything which moves the heart more, nor anything which drags grief [to the mind] more strongly than reading the Qur'an, understanding it and pondering over it."

A man, then, is affected by Qur'an-recitation by being charac-

236 Qur'an 20:82. 237 Qur'an 20:82. 238 Qur'an 103:1-3. 239 Qur'an 7:56.

terized by the quality of the verse recited. Thus when reading a verse which warns and restricts divine forgiveness to those who fulfil certain stipulations, he will make himself so small as if for fear he is about to die. When a verse on promise of forgiveness is recited he will rejoice as if he flies for [285] joy. When God, His attributes and names are mentioned, he will bow his head in submission to His majesty and in awareness of His greatness. When he reads a verse on the infidels' belief in an impossible thing for God (great and mighty is He!) — e.g. their belief that God (great and mighty is He!) has a child[240] and a consort —, he will lower his voice and be broken-hearted in bashfulness because of the evil[241] of what they have believed. When Paradise is described he will produce in his mind a yearning for it; but when Hell is described he will tremble for fear of it.

The Messenger of God (may God bless him and greet him!) once said to Ibn Mas'ūd, "Read the Qur'an to me." He said, "I started reading the Sura of Women (*Sura an-Nisā'*),[242] and when I reached the verse 'How will it be when [on the Day of Judgement] We shall bring a witness from every people, and shall bring you [i.e. Muḥammad] as a witness against these?' (فكيف اذا جئنا من كل امة بشهيد، وجئنابك على هوءلاء شهيدا),[243] I saw his eyes shedding tears. Then he said, 'Stop now' "[244] This is because thinking about the event which is referred to in this verse engrossed his mind fully. Among the fearers of God there are some who fell faint when reading verses about warnings. Some of them [even] died when hearing Qur'anic verses.

Mental states like these [just mentioned] will exclude the Qur'an-reader from being a mere narrator. When he says "Assuredly I fear, if I were to disobey my Lord, the punishment of an awful day" (انى اخاف، ان عصيت ربى، عذاب يوم عظيم),[245] but is not

240 The belief that God has a child is attributed in the Qur'an to Christians, Jews and pagans. For Christians Jesus is the son of God; for Jews Ezra ('Uzayr) is the son of God (Qur'an 9:30); pagan Arabs of pre-Islamic Arabia believed that their deities were angels whom they considered as daughters of God. Thus *walad* in Qur'anic contexts does not always mean 'son'; sometimes it means 'daughter'; sometimes it means both. The context will indicate what is meant in a specific verse and who are accused in it — Jews or Christians or pagans.

241 وينكسر فى باطنه حياء من قبح (BE: وينكسر فى باطنه حياء، قبح).

242 This is the fourth sura of the Qur'an consisting of one hundred and seventy-six verses.

243 Qur'an 4:41. 244 See *supra*, n. 151. 245 Qur'an 6:15.

[really] afraid of punishment, then he is a [mere] narrator of the verse. When he says "In You do we put our trust, to You do we turn in repentance, and to You is the final return" (عليك توكلنا ، واليك انبنا ، واليك المصير)[246] but has no mental states of trust and turning in repentance, then he is a [mere] narrator [of the words of this verse]. When he says, "We will surely continue steadfast under your persecution" (ولنصبرن على ما اذيتموانا),[247] his state should be that of steadfastness [against the opponent] or firmness in it so that he will find the sweetness of recitation. If he is not distinguished by these qualities and if his mind does not frequently experience these states, his part in Qur'an-recitation will [only] be the movement of the tongue [which is of no use] and which, moreover, brings an explicit curse on himself, as mentioned [a] in the words of God (exalted is He!), "Take notice, the curse of God is upon wrongdoers!" (الا لعنة الله على الظالمين!);[248] [b] in the words of God (exalted is He!), "Most hateful is it in the sight of God that you should say that which you do not do" (كبرمقتا عندالله ان تقولوا مالا تفعلون);[249] [c] in the words of God (great and might is He!), "Yet they are heedless and turn away" (وهم فى غفلة معرضون);[250] [d] in the words of God, "So turn away from him who turns away from the remembrance of Us, and seeks nothing except the life of this world" (فاعرض عمن تولى عن ذكرنا ولم يرد الا الحيواة الدنيا);[251] [e] in the words of God (exalted is He!), "Those who do not repent are those who are wrongdoers" (ومن لم يتب فأولئك هم الظالمون);[252] and in other verses. The Qur'an-reader will also be included in the meaning of [a] the words of God (great and mighty is He!), "Some of them are illiterate; they do not know the Book except *amāniyya*, (i.e. bare recitation of it)" (ومنهم اميون لا يعلمون الكتاب الا امانى)[253]; and [b] the words of God (great and mighty is He!), "How many signs there are in the heavens and in the earth which they pass by, turning away from them!" (وكأين من اية فى السموات والارض يمرون عليها وهم عنها معرضون).[254] The Qur'an-reader will be included in this verse because it is the Qur'an which explains these signs in the heavens and the earth and when he passes by them without being affected by them he is [in effect] turning away from them. For this reason it is said, "When a man who is not endowed with character-traits taught by the Qur'an reads

246 Qur'an 6:4.

247 Qur'an 14:12.

248 Qur'an 11:18.

249 Qur'an 61:3.

250 Qur'an 21:1. The complete verse is: "The time of reckoning is drawing near for people, yet they are heedless and turn away."

251 Qur'an 53:29.

252 Qur'an 49:11.

253 Qur'an 2:78.

254 Qur'an 12:105.

it, God (exalted is He!): asks: 'What is your relationship with My speech, seeing that you are turning away from Me? Leave aside My speech if you do not turn to Me in repentance.'"

A sinner, when he reads the Qur'an repeatedly is like one who [merely] reads the writing of the king several times every day; the king has written to him in order to make his kingdom prosperous, whereas he is engaged in ruining it and is content with [mere] study of what is written. Abandoning the study of it while at the same time opposing the king's order would not seem to be jesting with him and would not incur the hatred [of the king]. For this reason Yūsuf Ibn Asbāṭ said, "I certainly intend to read the Qur'an, but when I remember that which is in it I fear God's hatred and abandon it in favour of glorification of Him and praying for His forgiveness." Those who turn away from acting according to the Qur'an are intended in the words of God (great and mighty is He!), "They [i.e. those who were given the Book prior to the Qur'an] threw it [i.e. the covenant] away behind their backs and bartered it for a paltry price" (فنبذوهم وراء ظهورهم، واشتروا به ثمنا قليلا. فبئس ما يشترون)[255] For this reason the Messenger of God (may God bless him and greet him!) said, "Read the Qur'an so long as your minds are in agreement with it and your feelings are receptive to it. When you are in disagreement with it you are not [really] reading it." — in a certain Tradition [is this variation]: "When you are in disagreement with it stand up and stop reading it."[256] God (exalted is He!) said, "[Believers are only] those whose hearts are smitten with awe when God's name is mentioned and whose faith is strengthened when His signs are recited to them and who put their trust in their Lord" (الذين اذا ذكرالله وجلت قلوبهم واذا تليت عليهم اياته زادتهم ايمانا وعلى ربهم يتوكلون).[257] The Prophet (may God bless him and greet him!) said, "The best man in respect of reading the Qur'an is he whom, when you hear him reading it, you see fears God (exalted is He!)."[258] The Prophet (may God bless him and greet him!) said, "One cannot find a man to read the Qur'an who is more desirable than one who fears God (great and mighty is He!)."

Qur'an-reading,[259] then is intended to bring to the mind these states and to make one act in accordance with the Qur'an; otherwise

255 Qur'an 3:187.
256 Al-Bukhārī *Ṣaḥīḥ*, Faḍā'il al-Qur'an,37, I'tiṣām, 26; Muslim, *Ṣaḥīḥ*, 'Ilm, 3, 4; Ibn Ḥanbal, *Musnad*, IV, 313.
257 Qur'an 8:2, 258 Ibn Māja, *Sunan*, Iqāma, 176. 259 فالقرآن is omitted in BE.

the labour spent in moving the tongue with the sounds of the Qur'an is light. For this reason a certain Qur'an-reader said, "I read the Qur'an to my spiritual director (*shaykh*). After the completion of this reading when I returned to him in order to read it a second time, he rebuked me saying, 'You have made the reading of the Qur'an to me a set duty; go and read it to God (great and mighty is He!) — consider what are the duties He commands you to perform and what are the things He prohibits you.'" It is in this that [286] the Companions (may God be pleased with them!) were engaged in all conditions and actions. The Messenger of God (may God bless him and greet him!) died leaving [in Medina] twenty thousand Companions,[260] only six of whom memorized the Qur'an in its entirety; [even] in the case of two of these there is disagreement.[261] Most of the Companions used to memorize one sura or two. Anyone who could memorize the [Sura of the] Cow[262] and the [Sura of the] Cattle[263] was considered one of their scholars. One [of the Companions] once came [to the Prophet] to learn the Qur'an. [In the course of learning the Sura of the Earthquake,[264] when he reached the words of God (great and mighty is He!), "Whoever will have done the smallest particle of good will see it [on the Day of Judgement], and whoever will have done the smallest particle of evil will also see it" (فمن يعمل مثقال ذرة خيرا يره، ومن يعمل مثقال ذرة شرا يره),[265] he said, "This will suffice me" and returned home. The Prophet (may God bless him and greet him!) said, "This

260 The total number of companions of the Prophet when the latter died was one hundred and fourteen thousand, of whom twenty thousands were in Medina. See az-Zabīdī, *op. cit.*, IV, 522.

261 The four companions of the Prophet who are unanimously considered to have memorized the entire Qur'an during the Prophet's lifetime are Ubayy Ibn Ka'b, Mu'ādh Ibn Jabal, Zayd Ibn Thābit, and Abū Yazīd — all from the Helpers (*Anṣārs*) (al-Bukhārī, *Ṣaḥīḥ*, Faḍā'il al-Qur'an, 8). The two companions concerning whose memorization of the Qur'an in its entirety there is disagreement are: Abū d-Dardā' and Sa'īd Ibn 'Ubayd. See az-Zabīdī, *op. cit.*, IV, 522.

262 This is the second sura of the Qur'an consisting of two hundred and eighty-six verses. It includes the well known Verse of the Throne (2:255).

263 This is the sixth sura of the Qur'an. It consists of one hundred and sixty-five verses.

264 In the *muṣḥaf* of 'Uthmān, this is the ninety-ninth sura of the Qur'an. It consists of eight short verses. There is a Tradition that this sura is equal to a fourth part of the Qur'an in respect of value. See Ibn Ḥanbal, *Musnad*, III, 147, 221.

265 Qur'an 99:8.

man returned being one who has acquired the understanding of religion (*faqīh*)." [266] Assuredly a rare thing is that state which God (great and mighty is He!) bestows by favour upon a believer's mind just after his understanding [the meaning of] a verse. As for the mere movement of the tongue in recitation, it is of little benefit. Rather, one who recites the Qur'an with the tongue but turns away from acting [in accordance with it] is fit to be intended [a] in the words of God (great and mighty is He!), "Anyone who turns away from My Reminder [i.e. the Qur'an] will have a hard life, and on the Day of Judgement We shall raise him blind" (ومن اعرض عن ذكرى فان له معيشة ضنكا، ونحشره يوم القيامة اعمى),[267] and [b] in the words of God, "Thus it is. Our signs came to you and you forgot them; in like manner will you be forgotten on this day" (كذالك اتتك اياتنا فنسيتها، و كذالك اليوم تنسى).[268] "You forget them" means you abandoned them, did not look at them, and did not care about them, since to fall short of an affair is said to have forgotten it.

Recitation of the Qur'an in its real sense is an activity in which the tongue, the intellect and the mind all take part. The part which the tongue plays consists in correct pronunciation of letters in a slow and distinct manner. The part played by the intellect lies in explaining the meanings. The part which the mind plays is to accept the exhortation given and to feel as a result of being checked [against the forbidden things] and obeying the commandments. Thus the tongue is the exhorter, the intellect is the translator [of what it understands of the exhortation], and the mind is that which accepts the exhortation.

[9]

The ninth mental task is the Qur'an-reader's gradually rising to [a state in which he feels that he is] hearing the speech of God from God (great and mighty is He!) and not from himself.

The grades of Qur'an-reading are three in number. The lowest grade is when a man supposes that he is reading the Qur'an to God (great and mighty is He!), standing in front of Him, and He is looking at him and listening to what he is reading. In this case his mental condition is one of begging [to God], praising and entreating Him and supplicating to Him.

266 Abū Dāwūd, *Sunan*, Ramaḍān, 9; Ibn Ḥanbal, *Musnad*, II, 169.

267 Qur'an 20:124.

268 Qur'an 20:126.

The second grade is when a man views with his mind that God (great and mighty is He!) is seeing him, addressing him with his kindnesses, and secretly conversing with him with his gifts and beneficence. So his station is one of modesty, magnification, listening and understanding.

The third grade is when a man [feels that he] is seeing the Speaker [i.e. God] in the speech [i.e. the Qur'an] and His attributes in its sentences. He does not think of himself, nor his Qur'an-reading, nor the relation of divine gifts to him as the one upon whom they are bestowed; rather he confines his care to the Speaker, and concentrates his thought on Him as if he were engrossed in the vision of the Speaker, being divested of thought of anything other than Him. This is the grade of those drawn near to God (*al-muqarrabūn*), while the grades preceding it [i.e. the first grade and the second grade] constitue the grades of people on the right (*aṣḥāb al-yamīn*); all grades other than these [three] form the grades of inattentive people (*al-ghāfilūn*).[269]

It is of the highest grade of Qur'an-reading that Ja'far Ibn Muḥammad aṣ-Ṣādiq[270] (may God be pleased with him!) reported when he said, "I swear by God, certainly God (great and mighty is He!) has revealed Himself to men in His speech, but they do not see Him." Once Ja'far experienced an ecstatic state in his ritual prayer so that he fell faint; when he recovered he was told what happened and was asked by people concerning its cause; he replied, "I was constantly repeating in my mind the Qur'anic verse [which I was reading in that ritual prayer] until I heard it from its Speaker, [287] and then my body could not remain steady because I saw His power." It is at a grade like this that the sweetness of Qur'an-reading and the pleasure of secret conversation with God become intense. For this reason a certain wise man said, "I used to read the Qur'an but did not find the sweetness of it until I recited it as if I were hearing it from the Messenger of God (may God bless him and greet him!) reciting to his companions. Then rising to a stage higher

269 These three groups of people represent al-Ghazālī's classification of believers especially. For the Qur'anic classification of man in general see *supra*, n. 37.

270 Imām Ja'far aṣ-Ṣādiq was the sixth of the twelve Imāms of the Shī'ites. He succeeded his father, Muḥammad al-Bāqir, as Imām. He played no part in politics. He was celebrated for his piety and asceticism, and for his knowledge of Tradition and a few other intellectual disciplines. He died in Medina in 148 A.H./756 A.D. See an-Nawawī, *op. cit.*, I, 149f.

than this I used to[271] recite the Qur'an as if I were hearing it from [the angel] Gabriel (may peace be upon him!) who was delivering it to the Messenger of God (may peace be upon him!). Then God brought me to another stage — I now hear it from its Speaker; at this stage I found in the Qur'an such intense pleasure and delight that I could not restrain myself.

'Uthmān and Ḥudhayfa (may God be pleased with them both!) said, "If men's souls are purified [from evil qualities] they will not be fully satisfied with Qur'an-reading; [rather some thirst for it will always remain]. They said this only because it is by purification [from evil qualities] that the soul rises to the stage of viewing the Speaker in His speech and His attributes in its sentences. For this reason Thābit al-Bunānī[272] said, "For twenty years I struggled [against my lower soul in order to attain] the Qur'an [at its highest grade] and [then] for twenty years I enjoyed the delight of it." By viewing the Speaker alone — besides all else — [in His speech] a man fully obeys the words of God (great and mighty is He!), "Then flee to God" (ففروا الى الله),[273] and His (exalted is He!)[274] words, "Do not set up any other god along with God"(ولا تجعلوا مع الله الها اخر).[275] One who does not see God in everything sees something other than Him, and if there is something other than God to which a man gives attention, this attention involves an element of hidden polytheism (*ash-shrik al-khafī*). Rather pure monotheism (*at-tawḥīd al-khāliṣ*) consists in seeing only God (great and mighty is He!) in everything.

[10]

The tenth mental task consists in the Qur'an-reader's getting rid of any sense of his ability and power[276] and his looking at himself with the eye of satisfaction and purification.[277]

When the Qur'an-reader recites verses on promise to, and praise

271 فكنت (BE: كنت).

272 Abū Muḥammad Thābit Ibn Aslam al-Bunānī (d. 123 or 127 A.H.), a native of Basra, was a celebrated Follower and a trustworthy transmitter of Tradition. He undertook self-training and mortification (*riyāḍa wa mujāhada*) in the recitation of the Qur'an. See Ibn Ḥajar al-'Asqalānī, *Tahdhīb at-Tahdhīb*, Hyderabad, India, 1325-27 A.H., II, 2ff.

273 Qur'an 51:50.

274 تعالى is omitted in BE.

275 Qur'an 51:51.

276 This is based on the Qur'anic verse 18:39.

277 Ascription of purity to oneself is prohibited in the Qur'anic verse (53:32): "So do not ascribe purity to yourselves. He [i.e. God] knows best him who is truly religious."

of, the pious he will not view himself as one of these; rather he will view those who have the most certain faith and those who are the most truthful in religion [i.e. the most devout] and will hope that God (great and mighty is He!) will join him with them [by raising him to their spiritual status]. When he recites verses on divine hatred and divine reproach of the disobedient and those falling short of [religious duties] he will view himself here and, fearing and pitying, will suppose that he is the man addressed and intended in these verses. For this reason 'Abd Allāh Ibn 'Umar (may God be pleased with them both!) used to say in his prayer, "God, I seek the forgiveness of You for my injustice and infidelity." He was asked, "[The meaning of this injustice is clear, but] what is the meaning of infidelity here?" In reply he recited the words of God (great and mighty is He!), "Surely man is very unjust and ungrateful" (ان الانسان لظلوم كفار).[278]

Yūsuf Ibn Asbāṭ was asked, "What do you pray for when you read the Qur'an?" He replied, "What I pray for is that I seek the forgiveness of God (great and mighty is He!) for my shortcoming [in Qur'an-reading] seventy times." Since he saw himself as one with shortcomings in Qur'an-reading, this became a cause of his nearness to God. For the man who views his 'distance'[279] from God when in a state of nearness [to Him] is shown [by Him] 'kindness' in his state of fear [of Him] so that his fear leads him to another degree of nearness beyond the existing one. But he who views his nearness [to God] while in fact being distant [from Him] is 'deceived' by a sense of 'security' [against God] which takes him even further [from God] and lower than his present position.

Whenever a man sees himself with the eye of satisfaction he becomes veiled from God by himself. When, however, he crosses the limit of looking at himself and does not see in his Qur'an-reading anything except God (exalted is He!), then the secret of the invisible world is revealed to him directly. Abū Sulaymān ad-Dārānī (may God be pleased with him!) said, "Ibn Thawbān promised his brother [in respect of religion] to break his fast with him [at sunset], but he delayed until dawn. Next day his brother met him and

278 Qur'an 14:34.

279 The terms distance (*bu'd*), kindness (*luṭf*), deception (*makr*), security (*amn*) and veil (*ḥijāb*), or their derivatives occur in the Qur'an several times. In ṣūfism they have acquired additional significance and are used as technical terms.

complained, "You promised me to break your fast with me and then broke the promise." He replied, "Had I not made a promise to you I would not have informed you of what prevented me from going to you. [What prevented me was that] on performing the Evening Prayer (*al-'atama*) I said to myself that I should perform the Odd Prayer (*Ṣāla al-Witr*)[280] before going to you, since I did not feel secure against the possibility of being overtaken by death. When I became engaged in the supplication formula[281] of the Odd Prayer I felt I was being lifted to a green meadow where there were different types of flowers from Paradise. I was constantly looking at them until the day-break."

These mystical intuitions can only occur after one gets rid of one's self and does not look at one's self with a sense of satisfaction and purification, nor at one's passion. Then these intuitions become specific in accordance with the mental state of the man receiving them. Thus when he recites verses on hope, and his mental state is dominated by a good omen from them, the image of Paradise comes to him through mystical intuition, as in the case of Ibn Thawbān just mentioned, and he views it as if he sees with his eyes. But if fear dominates him [as a result of reading verses on punishment], then Hell is shown to him through intuition so that he sees its different types of punishment. This is because the speech of God (great and mighty is He!) includes those verses which are kind and witty as well as those which are violent and forceful, and those which inspire hope as well as those which are frightening. And this is in accordance with God's attributes, since among His attributes are mercy and kindness as well as revenge and violence. Then, in accordance with the Qur'an-reader's view of Qur'anic sentences and of divine attributes, his mind alternates[282] in different mental states [e.g. between the

280 The Evening Prayer is the ritual prayer which is performed after the expiry of the time fixed for the ritual prayer performed immediately after sunset. The period during which it can be performed extends until dawn, but to delay it later than the first third of the night is disliked (*makrūh*) by the Sharī'a. The Odd Prayer consists of three *rak'as* and is performed after the Evening Prayer; its time also extends until dawn; it is however, better to postpone its performance until after midnight if one is sure to wake up at that time — better because a high degree of concentration on devotion can be achieved at that time and because it can be joined with the Tahajjud Prayer, a supererogatory ritual prayer to be performed immediately after midnight.

281 This supplication formula, together with its English translation, is cited in full in Quasem, *Salvation*, p.

282 القلب. يتقلب القلب is omitted in BE.

state of fear and the state of hope], and, according to each of these mental states, the mind is prepared for a mystical intuition appropriate to it and approaching it, since it is impossible that the mental state[283] of the listener will be different from that [i.e. the Qur'an] which he heard, for in it are the speech of One pleased, the speech of One angry, the speech of the Beneficent, the speech of the Avenger, the speech of the Most Powerful, the Arrogant Who need not care [for anyone], and the speech of the Compassionate, the Sympathiser Who does not neglect [anyone].

283 حال (BE: حالة).

CHAPTER FOUR

UNDERSTANDING THE QUR'AN, AND ITS EXPLANATION BY PERSONAL OPINION WHICH HAS NOT COME DOWN BY TRADITION

قال رسول الله' صلى الله عليه وسلم: من فسر القرأن برائه فليتبوء مقعده من النار.

Whoever explains the Qur'an according to his [wrong] personal opinion shall take his place in Hell. — prophet Muḥammad

The Problem

You may perhaps ask: In the preceding section you have magnified the matter concerning the understanding of deep meanings of the Qur'an (*asrār al-Qur'an*) and concerning those meanings of it which are unveiled (*yunkashif*) to people possessed of purified souls (*arbāb al-qulūb az-zakiyya*) [288]; how can this be praiseworthy seeing that the Prophet (may God bless him and greet him!) has said, "The man who explains the Qur'an according to his personal opinion (*bi-ra'yihi*) shall take his place in Hell?" [284] [Because of this prophetic Tradition] people expert in the outward exegesis of the Qur'an (*ẓāhir at-tafsīr*) have reviled the ṣūfīs, i.e. those exegetes [285] who subscribe to ṣūfism, and who [286] interprete (*ta'wīl*) certain Qur'anic sentences contrary to the explanations given by Ibn 'Abbās and other exegetes; the revilers maintain that these interpretations [lead to] infidelity. If what the proponents of outward exegesis have said is correct, what is the meaning of understanding the Qur'an without memorizing their exegesis? If [on the other hand] what they have said is not correct, what is the meaning of the Prophet's statement, "The man who explains the Qur'an according to his personal opinion shall take his place in Hell?"

284 At-Tirmidhī, *Sunan*, Tafsīr, 1. 285 المفسرين (BE and MH: المقصرين).

286 E.g. Abū 'Abd ar-Raḥmān as-Sulamī, Abū Naṣr as-Sarrāj, al-Qushayrī, and

Existence of Deep, Hidden Meanings of Qur'anic Verses

[In reply to your question] know that the man who imagines that the Qur'an has no meaning except that which the outward exegesis has translated [and described] is acknowledging his own limitations; he is right in his acknowledgement [because he knows only this measure and is not aware of that which lies beyond this], but is wrong in his judgement which places all other people on the same level as himself.

The truth is that prophetic Traditions (*akhbār*) and statements of the Prophet's companions and of other pious Muslims in early Islam (*āthār*) prove that for men of understanding there is wide scope in the meanings of the Qur'an. Thus 'Alī (may God be pleased with him!) said, "except that God bestows understanding of the Qur'an upon a man."[287] If there is no meaning other than that which is related [from Ibn 'Abbās and other exegetes] what is that understanding of the Qur'an [which is bestowed upon a man]? The Prophet (may God bless him and greet him!) said, "Surely the Qur'an has an outward aspect, an inward aspect, a limit and a prelude." This is also related by Ibn Mas'ūd on his own authority and he is one of the scholars of Qur'anic explanation. [If there are no meanings of the Qur'an besides the outward ones], what is the meaning of its outward aspect, inward aspect, limit and prelude? 'Alī (may God show regard to his face!) said, "If I so will I can certainly load seventy camels with the exegesis of the Opening Sura of the Book." What then is the meaning of this statement of 'Alī, when the outward exegesis of this sura is extremely short[288] [and can be set forth in a few pages]? Abu d-Dardā'[289] said, "One cannot [fully] understand the religion until one sees the Qur'an from different perspectives." A certain religious scholar said, "For every Qur'anic verse there are sixty thousand understandings [comprehensible to man]. The understandings of it which remain [incomprehensible to man] are even more than these in number." Another religious scholar said, "The Qur'an encompasses seventy-seven

al-Kāshānī. See az-Zabīdī, *op. cit.*, IV, 526; Muhammad Abul Quasem, "Al-Ghazālī in Defence of Ṣūfistic Interpretation of the Qur'an", sec. i (forthcoming).

287 This saying of 'Alī is cited in its full form in the preceding chapter.

288 الاقتصار (LN: الاختصار).

289 Abū d-Dardā' 'Uwaymar al-Anṣārī (d. 32 A.H.), a companion of the Prophet, embraced Islam in 2 A.H. and was praised by the Prophet for his vigorous fighting at Uḥud (3 A.H.). On another occasion the Prophet called him "the wise man (*hakīm*) of

thousand and two hundred forms of knowledge, since every Qur'anic sentence constitutes one form of knowledge. This number is multiplied by four times, since each sentence has its outward aspect, inward aspect, limit and prelude. Repetition of the verse, "In the name of God, most Gracious, Ever Merciful"(بسم الله الرحمن الرحيم),[290] by the Prophet (may God bless him and greet him!) twenty times could not have been for any reason other than that he was pondering over its deep, inward meanings; otherwise its translation and its outward exegesis are so obvious that one like the Prophet would not be in need of repetition. Ibn Mas'ūd (may God be pleased with him!) said, "One who intends to acquire [the core principles of] the knowledge of the ancients and the moderns should ponder over the Qur'an. This knowledge is something which is not achieved by its mere outward exegesis.[291]

In short, all forms of knowledge are included in the works of God (great and mighty is He!) and His attributes, and in the Qur'an there is an explanation of His essence, attributes and works. These forms of knowledge have no end, but in the Qur'an there is an indication (*ishāra*) of their confluence. Penetrating deeply into the explanation of the Qur'an by stages amounts to the understanding of the Qur'an; mere outward exegesis[292] does not lead to that. The truth is that to everything pertaining to reflective and intellectual matters which has become ambiguous to men of reflection and in which people have differed, there are indications and implications in the Qur'an which can be grasped by men of understanding. How can these indications and implications be completely conveyed by the translation of its outward meanings and by its [outward] exegesis?

This is the reason why the Prophet (may God bless him and greet him!) ordered, "Read the Qur'an and seek to know its [deep], strange meanings [by eliciting and understanding]." He (may God bless him and greet him!) also said, in a Tradition related by 'Alī (may God show regard to his face!), "I swear by Him Who has sent me as a prophet in accordance with the requirements of truth and wisdom, surely my community will be split up into seventy-two sects all of which are misguided[293] themselves and misguide others by calling them to Hell. When this state of affairs comes about you

my community." He transmitted many Traditions. See Ibn Ḥajar, *op. cit.*, III, 46.

290 Qur'an 1:1. 291 تفسره الظاهر (BE: تفسير الظاهر).

293 ضاله (LN: ضلاله). 292 ظاهر التفسير (BE: ظاهره التفسير).

must adhere to the Book of God (great and mighty is He!), for in it lies the message concerning those who were before you and the message concerning what will happen after you, and the judgement of all that happens among you. Anyone of [even] the most powerful men who contradicts it is severely punished by God (great and mighty is He!), anyone who seeks knowledge from a source other than it is led astray by God (great and mighty is He!). It is the strong rope of God [which man should grasp firmly], His clear light [in which man should walk in all aspects of his life], and His useful means of healing [of man's spiritual diseases];[294] it is a protection for one who holds fast to it, and a [means of] salvation for one who follows it; it is not distorted so that it needs to be set aright, nor has it deviated so that it needs to be brought to its normal state; its wonders are never exhausted, nor does much-repeated recitation of it make it old." [289] — to the end of the Tradition.[295] In a Tradition narrated by Ḥudhayfa it is mentioned that when the Messenger of God (may God bless him and greet him!) informed him of the disagreements [among Muslims] and their splitting into sects which would occur after his time, he said, "I enquired, 'Messenger of God, what do you command me to do should I meet with that [unfortunate state of affairs]?' He replied, 'Learn the Book of God, and act in accordance with its teachings. This is the way of escaping from that [state of affairs].' " Ḥudhayfa said, "I repeated that question to the Prophet thrice, and he replied thrice by saying, 'Learn the Book of God (great and mighty is He!) and act in accordance with what is taught in it, for in its lies salvation.' "[296]

'Alī (may God show regard to his face!) said, "One who understands the Qur'an can thereby explain the totality of knowledge." By this statement 'Alī indicated that the Qur'an implies the confluence of all forms of knowledge. [Abd Allāh] Ibn 'Abbās (may God be pleased with them both!) said, in the explanation of the words of God (exalted is He!), "Whoever is granted wisdom has indeed been granted abundant good"(ومن يوت الحكمة فقد اوتى خيرا كثيرا),[297] that "abundant good" means understanding of the Qur'an. God (great and mighty is He!) said, "We gave Solomon the right understanding of the matter, and upon each [of David and Solomon] We bestowed

294 Qur'an 17:82.

295 At-Tirmidhī, *Sunan*, Īmān, 18; Abū Dāwūd, *Sunan*, Sunna, 1; Ibn Māja, *Sunan*, Fitan, 17 (with variation).

296 Abū Dāwūd, *Sunan*, Sunna, 28.

297 Qur'an 2:269.

wisdom and knowledge" (ففهمنا ها سليمان، وكلا اتينا حكما وعلما).[298] Here God has called what He bestowed upon both Solomon and David "knowledge and wisdom," but the prudence which He gave Solomon alone He explicitly mentioned as "right understanding" and mentioned it before "wisdom and knowledge".

The matters [mentioned above], then, prove that in the understanding of the meanings of the Qur'an there is a wide range and excessive width and that outward exegesis which has come down by tradition is not the end of the understanding of the Qur'an.

The Prophet's Prohibition of Qur'an-explanation according to One's Personal Opinion

As for the saying of the Prophet (may God bless him and greet him!), "The man who explains the Qur'an according to his personal opinion... ,"[299] and his (may God bless him and greet him!) prohibition of this kind of Qur'anic explanation, the saying of Abū Bakr (may God be pleased with him!), "What earth will bear me and what sky will over-shadow me if I say anything by my personal opinion when explaining the Qur'an?," and other prophetic traditions and statements of the Prophet's companions and of other pious Muslims in early Islam on the prohibition of Qur'anic explanation by personal opinion — these were intended [a] either to confine the understanding of the Qur'an to that which has come down by tradition (*naql*) and to that which is heard [from authorities on exegesis] (*masmū'*) and to abandon the eliciting [of meanings from the texts of the Qur'an (*istinbāṭ*)[300] and independent understanding (*istiqlāl*), or [b] to be something different. It is certainly wrong to believe that the purpose was to limit our understanding of the Qur'an to only that which one hears and receives from an authority; and [this is wrong] for serveal reasons:

First, it is a stipulation that it should be heard from the [mouth of the] Messenger of God (may God bless him and greet him!) and be supported by a chain of narration going back to him, but this is something which applies only in the case of [a small] part of the Qur'an. As for the [explanation of the Qur'an] which Ibn 'Abbās and Ibn Mas'ūd give from their own understanding, it should not be

298 Qur'an 21: 79.

299 At-Tirmidhī, *Sunan*, Tafsīr, 1. This Tradition in its full form is cited in the first paragraph of this chapter.

300 Cf. Qur'an 4:83.

accepted and should be called 'an explanation of the Qur'an by personal opinion,' because they have not heard this explanation from the Messenger of God (may God bless him and greet him!). The same is true of other Companions (may God be pleased with them!): [They too gave explanations of certain Qur'anic words, without hearing them from the Prophet; so their explanations should also be regarded as explanations of the Qur'an by personal opinion].

Second, companions of the Prophet and exegetes [who flourished after them] disagreed over the explanation of some Qur'anic verses; they gave such varying explanations of them that it is impossible to reconcile them. It is impossible that all these conflicting explanations were heard from the Messenger of God (may God bless him and greet him!); if one of them was in fact heard the rest [which are contradictory to it] must be rejected. Thus it is definitely clear that on the meaning [of words of the Qur'an] every exegete came to his own conclusions through his eliciting, [investigation and personal effort], so that they gave seven different opinions concerning the letters at the start of some suras which are impossible to reconcile. Thus a certain exegete said that *alif lām rā* (الر)[301] are letters from the word *ar-Raḥmān* (الرحمن). Another said that the letter *alif* (ا) stands for *Allāh* (الله), the letter *lām* (ل) for *laṭīf* (لطيف), and the letter *rā* (ر) for *Raḥīm* (رحيم); other exegetes gave other explanations. Since reconciliation of these explanations is impossible how can they all have been heard from the Prophet?

Third, the Prophet (may God bless him and greet him!) prayed for Ibn 'Abbās (may God be pleased with him!) saying, "God, bestow upon him the understanding of the religion and teach him the interpretation (*ta'wīl*) of the Qur'an." If interpretation of the Qur'an is something which is heard [from the Prophet] like revelation and which is preserved the way revelation is preserved, what is the sense in specifying Ibn 'Abbās in this case?

Fourth, God (great and mighty is He!) said, "Those of them who are adept at eliciting the truth would know its [real nature]" (لعلمه الذين يستنبطونه منهم).[302] In this verse God affirmed the validity of

301 These Arabic letters occur at the start of five Qur'anic suras — the tenth, eleventh, twelfth, fourteenth and fifteenth. Also see *supra*, n. 32.

302 Qur'an 4:83. This verse in full is: "When there comes to them any tidings bearing upon security or causing fear, they bruit it about; whereas if they were to refer it to the

eliciting meaning by men of learning. And it is well known that the eliciting of meaning is something beyond hearing [from an authority; it has to do with one's knowledge and understanding]. The totality of the statements of the Companions and other pious Muslims in early Islam on the understanding of the Qur'an which we have quoted [above] contradicts this opinion. Thus it is false that hearing [from an authority] is a stipulation for Qur'anic interpretation. It is lawful for everyone to elicit meaning from the Qur'an commensurate with his understanding and the limit of his intelligence.

Real Reasons for Prohibition of Qur'an-explanation according to One's Personal Opinion

As for the prohibition of explanation of the Qur'an by personal opinion, it is for one of two reasons. One of them is that the person giving an explanation has an opinion [of his own] on a matter, and this opinion is influenced by his nature (*ṭab'*) and passion (*hawā*). So he interprets the Qur'an according to his opinion (*ra'y*) and passion in order that he may adduce an argument in favour of his purpose — if he did not have that opinion and that passion that meaning would not appear to him from the Qur'an.[303] [This happens in different conditions.] [a] Sometimes it happens despite knowledge [of the Sharī'a], as in the case of a man who adduces an argument from a certain Qur'anic verse for validating his heresy (*bid'a*) knowing [well] that this is not intended in the verse, but by doing this he seeks to confuse his opponent.

[b] Sometimes it happens to a man ignorant [of the basic principles of the Sharī'a]. But since a Qur'anic verse can be interpreted [from two or more perspectives] his understanding inclines to that perspective which [290] suits his purpose and that aspect is given preponderance by his own opinion and passion. Thus it turns out that he has explained the verse with his personal opinion, i.e. his personal opinion is that which has led him to that explanation. If his own opinion did not exist the perspective [which suits his purpose, and not the other] would not bear such weight with him.

Messenger and to those in authority among them, surely those of them who are adept at eliciting the truth, would know its [real nature]."

303 This is the practice of Shī'ites, especially the Bāṭinities, Mu'tazilities, Qādiānīs, Aḥmadiyyas, and some of the modernists in different Muslim countries, concerning certain specific Qur'anic verses

[c] Sometimes a man has a valid purpose for which he seeks a proof from the Qur'an, and he adduces a proof for that purpose with[304] a verse in which, he knows, that purpose is not intended.[305] An example of this is a man who invites people to pray for forgiveness of God just before dawn and who adduces an argument for this from the words of the Prophet (may God bless him and greet him!), "Eat a meal just before dawn, for there is blessing in this meal."[306] He gives the impression to people that the intended purpose of this saying of the Prophet is remembrance of God just before dawn,[307] knowing well that the purpose really intended by this saying is to eat food [just before dawn]. Another example is a man who invites people to strive hard against hardness of the mind. He says that God (great and mighty is He!) ordered [Moses], "Go to Pharaoh; he has certainly transgressed grievously" (اذهب الى فرعون، انه طغى)[308], and, hinting at his own heart, say: 'This is what is meant by Pharaoh [in this verse]'. This kind [of Qur'anic explanation] is sometimes employed by some religious preachers for good purposes by embellishing their speeches and encouraging their audience [to these purposes], but this is forbidden. Sometimes Shi'a Bāṭinites employ this [kind of explanation of the Qur'an] for corrupt purposes in order to deceive people and to invite them to their false school of thought and practices (*madhhab*). To support their [corrupt] opinions and [false] school, they bring down the Qur'an to certain matters, knowing definitely that these matters are not meant in the Qur'an.[309]

These [three] kinds of explanations, then, constitute one of the two reasons for prohibition of Qur'an-explanation by personal opinion. The intended meaning of 'personal opinion' would be the corrupt personal opinion suitable to one's passion and not correct personal effort. Personal opinion includes that which is valid and that which is corrupt, and that which is affected by passion is sometimes specified with the name of personal opinion.

304 بما (BE: لما). 305 ماارید به, which is omitted in MH.

306 An-Nasā'ī, *Sunan*, Ṣiyām, 18, 19; Ibn Māja, *Sunan*, Ṣiyām, 22; Ibn Ḥanbal, *Musnad*, II, 377, 477, III, 32, 99.

307 Remembrance of God just before dawn is praised in the Qur'an 3:17.

308 Qur'an 20:24.

309 Al-Ghazālī wrote several books directed in whole or in part against the Shī'a Bāṭinites or Ta'līmites who were identical with Ismā'īlites and completely exposed the falsity of their heretical beliefs. See Quasem, *Jewels*, p. 39.

The second reason [for the prohibition of Qur'an-explanation by personal opinion] is that [this prohibition applies to] one who hastens to explain the Qur'an by considering the outward aspect [i.e. the rules] of the Arabic language without knowing by heart what was heard [from authorities] and transmitted [from them], in the cases of those verses which use strange Qur'anic words (*gharā'ib al-Qur'an*), in the case of those verses in which ambiguous terms and substitute words occur, and in the case of those verses in which are to be found conciseness, omission, suppression of words understood, precedence [of a word from its proper place] and putting a word at a place later [than the appropriate one]. One who, without being prudent at outward exegesis, hastens to elicit deep meanings by mere understanding the [rules of] the Arabic language makes many mistakes and is included in the group of those who explain the Qur'an by personal opinion. Then transmission [from an authority] and hearing [from him] are necessary for outward exegesis first, so that the exegete may, by them, be safe in places where mistakes are likely to be made. After this, understanding will be wide and the eliciting of deep meanings will be possible.

The strange words of the Qur'an[310] which can only be understood by hearing directly [from authorities] are many. We should like to indicate a number of them so that one may seek information about this type and know that it is not permissible to neglect the memorization of outward exegesis first. There is no coveted object in reaching the inward [knowledge] before being prudent at the outward. One who claims to possess understanding of the deep meanings of the Qur'an, without being prudent at its outward exegesis, is comparable to a man who claims to reach the upper part of a house without crossing its door, or claims to understand the purposes of the Turks from their speeches whereas he does not understand the language of the Turks. [This is] because outward exegesis occupies the place of learning the language which is needed for understanding [the meaning].

Several Qur'anic Subjects in which Transmission from Authorities on Qur'anic Exegesis is Necessary

There are many [Qur'anic] subjects in which hearing directly

310 A number of books on this subject has been produced by Muslim scholars (az-Zabīdī, *op. cit.* IV, 529). The best of all these works is ar-Rāghib al-Iṣfahānī's book *al-Mufradāt fī Gharīb al-Qur'an*.

[from authorities] is necessary. [a] One of them is conciseness by omission and suppression of words understood. Examples of this are as follows. [1] The words of God (exalted is He!), "واتينا ثمود الناقة مبصرة،فظلموا بها"[311] Its meaning is: اية مبصرة،فظلموا بقتلها (We gave Thamūd the she-camel as a clear sign; but they [i.e. his people] did wrong to themselves by killing it). The man who looks at the outward [i.e. the rules of] Arabic [of this verse] imagines that the intended meaning is that the she-camel had eyes and not blind. He also does not know by what [the people of Thamūd] did wrong and whether they did wrong[312] to others or to themselves.

[2] The words of God (exalted is He!), "واشربوا في قلوبهم العجل بكفرهم"[313] i.e. حب العجل (because of their disbelief their minds were filled with love of the calf). The word *ḥubb* (love) is omitted. [3] The words of God (great and mighty is He!), "اذا لاذقناك ضعف الحيواة وضعف الممات"[314] i.e. ضعف عذاب الاحياء وضعف عذاب الموتى (then [i.e. if you had inclined to the infidels but a little] We would have afflicted you with the intensified chastisement of those who are living and the intensified chastisement of those who have died). The words *al-aḥyā'* and *al-mawtā* are substituted by *al-ḥayāt* and *al-mawat*, and all this is permissible in eloquent language.

[4] The words of God (exalted is He!), "واسئل القرية التي كنا فيها و العير التي اقبلنا فيها"[315] i.e. اهل القرية واهل العير[316] (you ask the people of the city wherein we were and the caravan with which we travelled). Thus in both, the word *ahl* is omitted[317] and suppressed as a word understood. [5] The words of God (great and mighty is He!), "ثقلت في السموات والارض"[318]. Its meaning is: خفيت على اهل السموات والارض (it [i.e. the time of the Hour of the Doom] lies hidden to those who are in the heavens and the earth). Since a thing lies heavy (*thaqula*) if its knowledge lies hidden (*khafiya*) the word meaning hidden is substituted by the word meaning heavy, and the word *fī* (in) is put in the place of *'alā* (to), and the term *ahl* (those who) is suppressed as understood and omitted.

[6] The words of God (exalted is He!), "وتجعلون رزقكم انكم تكذبون"[319] i.e. شكر رزقكم (do you make it the gratitude of your sustenance that you consider [the Qur'an] as false? [7] The words of

311 Qur'an 17:59. 312 وانهم ظلموا, which is omitted in BE and MH. 313 Qur'an 2:93.
314 Qur'an 17:75. 315 Qur'an 12:82. التي اقبلنا فيها is omitted in ZE.
316 اهل القرية is omitted in BE.
317 فالا هل فيهما محذوف (ZE: والاهل محذوف). 318 Qur'an 7:87. 319 Qur'an 56:82.

God (great and mighty is He!), " اتنا ماوعدتنا على رسلك ,"[320] i.e. على السنة رسلك (Lord, grant us that which you have promised us through the tongues of Your messengers'). The word *alsina* (tongues) is omitted. [8] The words of God (exalted is He!), " انا انزلناه في ليلة القدر "[321] (surely We sent it [i.e. the Qur'an] down during the Night of Decrees). By "it" God meant the Qur'an, without mentioning it before.

[9] God (great and mighty is He!) said, " حتى توارت بالحجاب "[322] (until it [i.e. the sun] disappeared in the veil of the night). By "it" God intended the sun, without mentioning it earlier. [10] The words of God (exalted is He!), " والذين اتخذوا من دونه اولياء، مانعبدهم الا ليقربونا الى الله زلفى ,"[323] i.e. يقولون مانعبدهم (those who adopt patrons other than God [say]: We worship them only that they may bring us near to God).

[11] The words of God (great and mighty is He!), " فما لهؤلاء القوم لايكادون يفقهون حديثا؛ مااصابك من حسنة فمن الله، وما اصابك من سيئة فمن نفسك ."[324] Its meaning is: لايفقهون حديثا، يقولون: مااصابك من حسنة فمن الله (what ails these people that they do not even approach the understanding of a speech? [They said:] Whatever good comes to you is from God, and whatever ills befall you is from yourself). If this is not meant, these verses contradict the words of God[325] preceding them: "Tell them: All is from God"? (قل: كل من عند الله),[326] and the Qadarite school of thought[327] comes to this understanding.

[B] Among the Qur'anic subjects in which transmission [from authorities] is necessary is inversion. For example: [1] The words of God (exalted is He!), " وطور سينين ,"[328] i.e. طور سيناء (and the

320 Qur'an 3:194. 321 Qur'an 97:1.

322 Qur'an 38:32. This verse in full is: "He [i.e. Solomon] said, 'I preferred the good things [of the world] to the remembrance of my Lord until it [i.e. the sun] disappeared in the veil [of the night]." For more information see Qur'an 38:31-34.

323 Qur'an 39:3. 324 Qur'an 4:79-80. 325 لقوله, which is omitted in MH.

326 Qur'an 4:79.

327 This was an early heretical school of Islamic theology founded by Ma'bad al-Juhanī (d. 704 A.D.) It almost disappeared in the ninth century when its main doctrines were incorporated into Mu'tazilism. There were several groups of early Qadarites, one of which believed that all that is good is from God but all that is evil is from man himself (W. Montgomery Watt, *The Formative Period of Islamic Thought*, Edinburgh, 1973, p. 94). It is to this group that al-Ghazālī seems to have referred here. The standard Sunnite view held by al-Ghazālī is that God by His power determines all happenings and acts, including human acts.

328 Qur'an 95:2.

Mount [291] Sinai). [2] [The verse], " سلام على ال يا سين ," [329] i.e. على الياس (may peace be upon Elias!). Some authorities have said that Idrīs is meant here, because in the *muṣḥaf* of Ibn Mas'ūd is to be found: " سلام على ادراسين "[330] (may peace be upon Idrīs!).

[C] Among the Qur'anic subjects in which transmission [from authorities] is necessary is repetition which breaks the connection of speech. Examples are: [1] The words of God (great and mighty is He!), " وما يتبع الذين يدعون من دون الله شركاء. ان يتبعون الا الظن ".[331] It means: وما يتبع الذين يدعون من دون الله شركاء الا الظن [332] (those who call on others than God do not follow any associates of Him except their own conjecture). [2] The words of God (great and mighty is He!), " قال الملاء الذين استكبروا من قومه للذين استضعفوا لمن امن منهم ".[333] The meaning is: استكبروا لمن امن من الذين استضعفوا (those leading men of his people who were haughty spoke to the believers among those who were reckoned weak).

[D] Among the Qur'anic subjects in which transmission [from authorities] is necessary, is the occurrence of a word before or after its proper place. This is a place where error is made by people. Examples of this are: [1] The words of God (great and mighty is He!), " ولولا كلمة سبقت من ربك. لكان لزاما واجل مسمى ".[334] Its meaning is: ولولا الكلمة واجل مسمى. لكان لزاما (were it not for a word already gone forth from your Lord, and a term already fixed, their [i.e. disbelievers'] punishment would have been inevitable [in this world].) If this were not the meaning the last letter of the word *ajal* would have been marked with *fatḥa*, as in the case of the term *lizām*. [2] The words of God (exalted is He!), " يسئلونك كانك حفي عنها ,"[335] i.e. يسئلوانك عنها كانك حفي بها (they ask you concerning it [i.e. the Hour of Doom] as if you were well acquainted with it). [3] The words of God (great and mighty is He!), " لهم مغفرة ورزق كريم. كما اخرجك ربك من بيتك بالحق "[336] (to them [i.e. true believers] will be given forgiveness and honourable provision; as your Lord brought you [i.e. Muḥammad] forth from your house [to take up arms] in a righteous cause). [Parts of] this verse are disjoined; its [second part] turns to a preceding speech of God,[337] [and when joined with that speech it stands thus:] " قل الانفال لله والرسول. كما اخرجك ربك من بيتك بالحق ," i.e. booties of goats have come to you since you were pleased to come

329 Qur'an 37:130. 331 Qur'an 10:66. 333 Qur'an 7:75. 330 MH has: سلام على ادريس

332 وما يتبع الذين يدعون من دون الله شركاء الا الظن . This is omitted in BE and MH.

334 Qur'an 20:129. 335 Qur'an 7:187. 336 Qur'an 8:4-5. 337 Qur'an 8:1.

[from your house], while they [i.e. a party of the believers] were displeased. Between these words is put, as parenthesis, the command to fear God and to do other things. Of this type are the words of God (great and mighty is He!), "حتى تؤمنوا بالله وحده الا قول ابراهيم لابيه الاية"[338] (until you believe in God, the One; except Abraham's saying to his father...).

[E] Among the Qur'anic subjects in which transmission [from authorities] is necessary is an ambiguous expression (*mubham*). It is an expression with different meanings, and it may be a word or a letter. Examples of ambiguous words are: *ash-shya', al-qarīn, al-umma, ar-rūḥ*, and the like.

God (exalted is He!) said, "ضرب الله مثلا عبدا مملوكا لايقدر على شيىء"[339] (God sets forth the example of a slave who is owned by a person and has no power over anything). By the word *shay'* (anything) God meant spending out of the provision given to the slave. God (great and mighty is He!) said, "ضرب الله مثلا رجلين: احدهما ابكم لايقدر على شيىء"[340] (God sets forth the example of two men: One of them is dumb having no capacity for achieving anything). *Shay'* (anything) here means to enjoin justice and righteousness. God (great and mighty is He!) said, [reporting Khaḍir's[341] words to Moses], "فان اتبعتني فلاتسألني عن شيىء"[342] (if you would follow me ask me no question about anything). Here by *shay'* (anything) God meant Lordly attributes (*ṣifāt ar-rubūbiyya*), which[343] are those forms of knowledge about which it is not lawful to ask until the gnostic (*'ārif*) starts with them when he begins to be fit to receive it. God (great and mighty is He!) said, "ام خلقوا من غير شيىء، ام هم الخالقون؟"[344] (have they [i.e. disbelievers] been created by nothing, or are they their own creators)? *Shay'* (thing) here means creator. Sometimes it is [wrongly] supposed that this verse proves that a thing can only be

338 Qur'an 60:4. 339 Qur'an 16:75. 340 Qur'an 16:76.

341 Al-Khaḍir is generally believed to be a saint (*walī Allāh*). One day when the prophet Moses was preaching to the Children of Israel, he was asked if there was any man wiser than he. When he replied in the negative, God revealed to him that His pious 'servant' (*'abd*), i.e. al-Khaḍir, was wiser than he. (al-Bukhārī, *Ṣaḥīḥ*, 'Ilm, bāb, 16, 19, 44, Anbiyā', bāb, 27; Muslim, *Ṣaḥīḥ*, Faḍā'il, trad. 170-74; at-Trimidhī, *Sunan*, Tafsīr Sura 18, bāb, 1). Moses thereupon paid a visit to al-Khaḍir in order to learn from him the deep, hidden knowledge which God had bestowed upon him directly as a mercy (Qur'an 18:65). The conversation between Moses and al-Khaḍir is put in the Qur'an 18:60-82. For a discussion on al-Khadir see A.J. Wensinck, "Al-Khadir", *SEI*, pp. 232-35; aṭ-Ṭabarī, *Tārikh*, I, 188-94.

342 Qur'an 18:70. 343 هي (BE and MH: هو). 344 Qur'an 52:35.

created from a thing.

As for the word *qarīn* (companion), examples of its being ambiguous are: [1] The words of God (great and mighty is He!), "وقال قرينه: هذا مالدى عتيد. القيا فى جهنم كل كفار"[345] (his companion will say: I have here his record ready. [And the verdict will be:] Both of you, cast every infidel into Hell). By the word *qarīn* (companion) God has meant the angel to be entrusted with the infidel. [2] The words of God (exalted is He!), "قال قرينه: ربنا مااطغيته ولكن كان"[346] (his companion will say: Lord, I did not cause him to rebel against You; he was [far gone in error on his own]). By *qarīn* (companion) God has meant Satan.

As for the term *al-umma* it is applicable to eight meanings. *Al-umma* means: [1] A group of people, as in the words of God (exalted is He!), "وجد عليه امة من الناس يسقون"[347] (he [i.e. Moses] found around it [i.e. the spring of Midian] a group of people who were watering [their flocks]). [2] The followers of prophets, as in your saying 'نحن من امة محمد، صلى الله عليه وسلم' (we are from[348] the followers of Muḥammad — may God bless him and greet him!). [3] A man endowed with all forms of good and followed by others, as in the words of God (exalted is He!), "ان ابراهيم كان امة قانتا لله"[349] (Abraham was indeed endowed with all forms of good, humble for the sake of God). [4] Religion, as in the words of God (great and mighty is He!), "انا وجدنا اباءنا على امة"[350] (we have found our fathers holding to a certain religion). [5] Time and period, as in the words of God (great and mighty is He!), "الى امة معدودة"[351] (for a determined period); and in the words of God (great and mighty is He!), "وادكر بعد امة"[352] (and remembered after the lapse of a period). [6] Stature of a man. Thus it is said: 'So-and-so is of a good *umma*,' i.e. good stature. [7] A man who alone follows a religion —

345 Qur'an 50:23.   346 Qur'an 50:27.   347 Qur'an 28:23.

348 كقولك نحن من (BE and MH: كقولك عن).   349 Qur'an 16:120.   350 Qur'an 43:22.

351 Qur'an 11:8. The complete verse is: "If We hold back their [i.e. disbelievers'] punishment for a determined period, they most surely say: What holds it back?. Take notice, on the day when it will come upon them, it will not be averted from them; rather that which they used to mock shall encompass them."

352 Qur'an 12:45. The verse in full is: "He of the two [companions of the prophet Joseph in prison] who had been set free and who [now] remembered, after the lapse of a period, [that which had passed between Joseph and him], exclaimed: I can let you know [of a man in the prison who knows] the interpretation of the dream, so send me [to bring him here]." The story of Joseph is narrated in the Qur'an 12:21-101.

no one is his partner in following that religion. Thus the Prophet (may God bless him and greet him!) said, "Zayd Ibn 'Amr Ibn Nufayl will be resurrected alone as an *umma*."[353] [8] Mother. Thus it is said, 'This woman is the *umma* of Zayd,' i.e. mother of Zayd.

The term *rūḥ* has also occurred in the Qur'an in many meanings. We do not like to prolong [our discussion] by mentioning them.

[Just as ambiguity occurs in words] so also it occurs in letters. Examples of this are: [1] The words of God (great and mighty is He!), " فاثرن به نقعا فوسطن به جمعا ."[354] The first *hā'* alludes to *ḥawāfir* which are the *mūryāt*. The meaning is: They raised, with their hoofs, clouds of dust. The second *hā'* alludes to *ighāra* which is *al-mughīrāt subḥan fa-wasaṭna bihi jam'an*. [The meaning is:] The polytheists gathered together, and the raiders at dawn raided their gathering. [2] The words of God (exalted is He!), " فانزلنا به الماء فاخرجنابه من كل الثمرات "[355] (We send down water from it, and We bring forth with it fruits of every kind). The first *hā'* (it) refers to *as-saḥāb* (cloud) and the second *hā'* (it) to *al-mā'* (water). Cases like this are so many [in the Qur'an] that they cannot be counted.

[F] Among the Qur'anic matters in which transmission [from authorities] is necessary is progression in exposition. An example of this is the words of God, " شهر رمضان الذي انزل فيه القرأن "[356] (the month of Ramaḍān is the month in which the Qur'an began to be revealed). From this verse it has not become clear whether the start of revelation was at night or at daytime, but it has become clear from the words of God (great and mighty is He!), " انا انزلناه فى ليلة

353 Zayd Ibn 'Amr Ibn Nufayl, a Meccan and Quraysh, died about five years before the advent of Isam. He was a *ḥanīf*, a seeker of the true religion, the religion of the prophet Abraham in its purity which taught monotheism. Zayd had abandoned pagan religion without embracing either Christianity or Judaism, because these did not retain the purity of Abraham's religion. He transformed his monotheistic faith into action: He objected to the existing practice of female infanticide, and refused to eat the flesh of animals sacrificed to idols, or slaughtered without invoking the name of One God. Persecuted by his family on religious grounds, he travelled in search of the true religion as far as Mawsil, and visited Syria; in Maifa'a, in Balkh, a learned monk predicted to him the rise of a true prophet in Mecca. Zayd hurried back but was assaulted and killed by the Christians while crossing the region inhabited by the Lakhm tribe. According to another tradition Zayd had himself predicted Muḥammad's prophethood. Though he died before Islam, he died as a monotheist. His son, Sa'īd, was the first convert to Islam from the clan of 'Adī. See Ibn Hishām, *op. cit.*, I, 222-32; Ibn Qutayba, *op. cit.*, pp. 59, 154.

354 Qur'an 100:4-5. 355 Qur'an 7:57. 356 Qur'an 2:185.

مباركة "[357] (We certainly revealed it [i.e. the Qur'an] in a blessed night). From this verse it has not become clear which night it was, but it has become clear from His (exalted is He!) words, " انا انزلناه فى ليلة القدر "[358] (We certainly revealed it [i.e. the Qur'an] during the Night of Decrees).[359] Sometimes, considering the outward aspect of these verses, one imagines that there is disagreement among them.

This and the cases similar to this are included in those Qur'anic subjects in which only transmission and hearing [from authorities] are of avail. The Qur'an, from its beginning to its end, is not devoid of this kind of thing, because it was revealed in the language of the Arabs and so it included various characteristics of their speech, such as conciseness, prolongation, suppression of words understood, omission, substitution of one word by another, and occurrence of a word before or after its proper place, so that it may be able to silence the voice of the Arabs against it and be fully eloquent to them. Anyone who is content with understanding the outward aspect [i.e. the rules] of the Arabic language and who hastens to explain the Qur'an without knowing by heart the meaning transmitted [from the authorities] in these Qur'anic subjects, is designated as 'a man who explains the Qur'an by his personal opinion.' Such an explanation is: He understands the best known meaning of the term *umma* and so is naturally inclined to this meaning [when he finds the word used in a verse]; but when he finds it in another place he is inclined to this well known meaning which he heard [and understood from authorities] [292] and abandons a thorough study of the transmission of its many meanings. Perhaps this is what is prohibited [by the Prophet] and not the understanding of deep meanings of the Qur'an, as has already been discussed. When hearing [from authorities] is achieved in [these and] similar Qur'anic subjects, then one has mastered the outward exegesis of the Qur'an which is [merely] the translation of its words. This, however, is not sufficient for understanding the reality of the meanings of the Qur'an.

The distinction between the reality of the meanings of the Qur'an

357 Qur'an 44:3.

358 Qur'an 97:1.

359 The tremendous excellence of the Night of Decrees is put in Qur'anic verses (97:3-5); "The Night of Decrees is better than a thousand months. Therein descends angels and the Spirit [i.e. Gabriel] by the command of their Lord [with their Lord's decrees] concerning every matter. [It is all] peace, till the break of dawn."

and its outward exegesis can be understood from an example: God (great and mighty is He!) said, "وما رميت اذ رميت، ولكن الله رمى"[360] (you [i.e. Muḥammad] did not throw [the handful of gravel at the infidels' faces] when you threw it, but God threw it). The outward exegesis of this verse is clear. Its real meaning, however, is obscure, because it affirms throwing and negates it [at the same time], and these appear contradictory unless it is understood that he [i.e. Muḥammad] threw from one perspective and did not throw from another and that from the perspective from which he did not throw God (great and mighty is He!) threw. Likewise God (exalted is He!) said, "قاتلواهم، يعذبهم الله بايديكم"[361] (fight them; God will punish them at your hands). When it is they [i.e. believers] who are the fighters how can God (glorified is He!) be the One Who inflicts punishment? If God (exalted is He!) is the One Who inflicts punishment by moving their hands what is the sense in commanding them to fight? The real solution to this problem receives help from a vast ocean of forms of knowledge obtained through mystical intuition (*'ulūm al-mukāshafāt*]; outward exegesis is of no avail. This solution consists in knowing [first] the mode of the linkage between man's works and the power created in him and [then] the mode of linkage between this power and the power of God (great and mighty is He!), so that, after the clarification of many obscure matters, there will be unveiled to him the truth of His words (great and mighty is He!), "You did not throw when you threw, but God threw."

If one's entire life is spent seeking the unveiling of secrets of this meaning and that which is linked up with those matters which precede and those which follow it, one's life will perhaps be exhausted before fully knowing all[362] that follows that meaning. A study of the real meaning of every sentence of the Qur'an needs a duration like this. Part of the secret meanings of the Qur'an is certainly unveiled to those established in knowledge, in proportion to the abundance of different forms of their knowledge, the purity of their souls [from vices], the fullness of their motives in pondering

360 Qur'an 8:117. This verse refers to an act at Badr (2 A.H.), the first great battle in Islam. When the war was in its full course the Prophet took a handful of pebbles and threw it at the enemy, the Meccan infidels. As a miracle of the Prophet the pebbles hit the face of each infidel and resulted in the diminishing of his mental vigour against the Muslims. For the Qur'anic account of the battle of Badr see Qur'an 8:1-50.

361 Qur'an 9:14.

362 جميع, which is omitted in MH.

[over the Qur'an], and their isolation for seeking [its meaning]. For each of those established in knowledge there is a limit in rising to a grade higher. As for the full unveiling of all the secret meanings, there is no coveted object in it. 'If the ocean were to become the ink and trees the pens [for transcribing] the secrets of God's words which have no end, all the oceans would be exhausted before the words of God (great and mighty is He!) came to an end.'[363] From this perspective men differ in understanding [the secret meanings of the Qur'an] after sharing in the knowledge of outward exegesis, and it is necessary to understand first the outward exegesis.

An example of this is the understanding of a certain ṣūfī (*ba'd arbāb al-qulūb*) from the words of the Prophet (may God bless him and greet him!) during his prostration, "I seek the protection of Your pleasure from Your displeasure; I seek the protection of Your forgiveness from Your punishment; and I seek the protection of You against You. I am unable to praise You; You are as You have praised Yourself."[364] The Prophet, being commanded [by God]: واسجد واقترب [365] (prostrate and [thereby] achieve nearness to Me), [prostrated] and, when he attained this nearness during prostration, considered divine attributes and sought the protection of an attribute from another — pleasure and displeasure are two divine attributes. Then, when his nearness to God increased including in itself the first nearness, he rose to divine essence and said, "I seek the protection of You against You." Then, when his nearness to God increased further as a result of a thing of which he felt ashamed, i.e. to seek protection being on the bed of nearness, he took refuge with praise, saying: "I am unable to praise You." Then when he realized that this was a shortcoming he said: "You are as You have praised Yourself."[366]

These are thoughts exposed to those possessed of purified souls

363 Cf. Qur'an 18:109.

364 Muslim, *Ṣaḥīḥ*, Ṣalā, 222; an-Nasā'ī, *Sunan*, Isti'ādha, 62, Ṭahāra, 119; at Tirmidhī, *Sunan*, Da'wāt, 75, 112; Abū Dāwūd, *Sunan*, Ṣalā, 148; Ibn Māja, *Sunan*, Iqāma, 117.

365 Qur'an 96:19.

366 This is al-Ghazālī's citation of a certain ṣūfī's understanding of the Tradition under consideration. He himself has much deeper understanding of it, as indicated in the subsequent paragraph of the text. He briefly discusses this Tradition in his *Jawāhir*, p. 24. A ṣūfistic interpretation of this Tradition was also cited by as-Sarrāj in his *Luma'*, p. 113. Al-Ghazālī seems to be influenced by him.

BIBLIOGRAPHY

Abū Dāwūd, Sulaymān Ibn al-Ash'ash as-Sijistānī. *Sunan*. 2 vols. Cairo, 1935.

Al-Abyārī, Ibrāhīm. *Tārīkh al-Qur'ān,* Cairo, 1965.

'Arafat, W."Bilāl b. Rabāḥ". *Encyclopaedia of Islam* (new ed.), I, 1215.

Al-'Asqalānī, Ibn Ḥajar. *Tahdhīb at-Tahdhīb*. 12 in 6 vols. Hyderabad, India, 1325-27 A.H.

—. *Al-Iṣāba*. 4 vols. Egypt, 1358/1939.

Azad, Mawlana Abul Kalam. *Basic Consepts of the Quran.* Prepared by Syed Abdul Latif. Hyderabad, India, 1958.

Bakker, Dirk. *Man in the Qur'ān.* Amsterdam, 1965.

Barth, J. "Studien sur Kritik und Exegese des Qorāns." *Der Islam,* VI (1915-16), 113-48.

Al-Bayḍāwī, 'Abd Allāh. *Anwār at-Tanzīl wa Asrār at Ta'wīl.* Egypt, 1923.

Bell, Richard. "Who were the Ḥanīfs?" *Moslem World, XX* (1930), 120-24.

—. "The Origin of 'Īd al-Aḍḥā". *Ibid.*, XXIII (1933), 117-20.

Birkeland, Harris. *The Lord guideth: studies on primitive Islam.* Oslo, 1956.

Al-Bukhārī, Muḥammad Ibn Ismā'īl. *Ṣaḥīḥ*. 9 vols. Egypt, 1377 A.H.

Carra de Vaux, B. "Yaḥyā", *Shorter Encyclopaedia of Islam*, p. 640.

Causse, Maurice. "Théologie de rupture et de la communauté: étude sur la vocation prophétique de Moïse d'après le Coran". *Revue de l'histoire et de la philosophie religieuses,* I (1964), 60-82.

Coulson, Noel J. *Conflict and Tensions in Islamic Jurisprudence*, Chicago, 1969.

Cragg, Kenneth. *The Event of the Qur'ān*. London, 1971.

—. *The Mind of the Qur'ān*. London, 1973.

Darrāj, Muḥammad 'Abd Allāh. *An-Nabā' al-'Aẓīm*. Egypt. 1379/1960.

Adh-Dhahabī, Abū 'Abd Allāh Muḥammad. *Tadhkira al-Ḥiffāẓ*. 4 vols. Hyderabad, India, 1333-34 A.H.

Adh-Dhahabī, Muḥammad Ḥusayn. *At-Tafsīr wa l-Mufassirūn*. 3 vols. Cairo, 1381/1961.

Fahd, T. "Ibn Sīrīn". *Encyclopaedia of Islam* (new ed.), III, 947-48.

Faris, Nabih Amin. "The Iḥyā' 'Ulūm al-Dīn of al-Ghazzālī." *Proceedings of the American Philosophical Society*, LXXI (1939), 15-19.

Al-Fīrūzābādī, Abū Ṭāhir Muḥammad Ibn Ya'qūb. *Tanwīr al-Miqyās min Tafsīr Ibn 'Abbās*. 2nd ed. Egypt. 1370/1901.

—. *Al-Qāmūs al-Muḥīṭ*. 4 vols. 3rd ed. Cairo, 1344/1925.

Gabrieli, F. "Adab". *Encyclopaedia of Islam* (new ed.), I, 175f.

Gardet, L. "Al-Asmā' al-Ḥusnā." *Encyclopaedia of Islam* (new ed.), I, 714-17.

Al-Ghazālī, Abū Ḥāmid. *Al-Arba'īn fī Uṣūl ad-Dīn*. Egypt, 1344 A.H.

—. *Iḥyā' 'Ulūm ad-Dīn*. 5 vols. Beirut, n.d.

—. *Jawāhir al-Qur'ān*. 2nd ed. Cairo, 1933.

—. *Al-Qisṭās al-Mustaqīm*. Edited by al-Yasū'ī. Beirut, 1959.

Al-Hujwīrī, 'Alī Ibn 'Uthmān. *Kashf al-Maḥjūb*. Translated by R.A. Nicholson. Leyden, 1911.

Ibn 'Abd al-Barr. *Al-Istī'āb*. In al-'Asqalānī, Ibn Ḥajar. *Al-Iṣāba*. 4 vols. Egypt, 1358/1953.

Ibn Abū Dāwūd, Abū Bakr 'Abd Allāh. *Kitāb al-Maṣāḥīf*. Edited by Arthur Jeffery. Egypt, 1355/1936.

Ibn al-Athīr. *Usd al-Ghāba*. 5 vols. Egypt, 1280 A.H.

Ibn al-Ḥajjāj, Muslim. *Ṣaḥīḥ*. 16 vols. Cairo, 1929.

Ibn Ḥanbal, Aḥmad. *Musnad*. 6 vols. Cairo, n.d.

Ibn al-Jawzī, 'Abd ar-Raḥmān. *Zād al-Masīr fī 'Ilm at-Tafsīr*. 6 vols. Beirut, 1384/1964.

Ibn Hishām. *As-Sīra an-Nabawiyya*. 2 vols. Edited by Muṣṭafā as-Saqā *et al*. 2nd ed. Egypt, 1955/1375.

Ibn Māja, Muḥammad Ibn Yazīd al-Qazwīnī. *Sunan*. 2 vols. Edited by Muḥammad Fu'ād 'Abd al-Bāqī. Cairo, 1952-53.

Ibn al-Manẓūr, Jamāl ad-Dīn Muḥammad Ibn Mukarram al-Anṣāri. *Lisān al-'Arab*. 20 vols. Cairo, 1308/1901.

Ibn an-Nadīm, Muḥammad. *Kitāb al-Fihrist*. Edited and translated by Bayard Dodge. 2 vols. New York & London, 1970.

Ibn Qutayba. *Al-Ma'ārif*. Edited by Tharwat 'Ukāsha. Cairo, 1969.

Ibn Taymiyya, Taqī ad-Dīn. *Muqaddama fī Uṣūl at-Tafsīr*. Edited by 'Adnān Zarzūr. 2nd ed. Beirut, 1392/1972.

—. *At-Tawassul wa l-Wasīla*. Beirut, 1390/1970.

Al-Iṣfahānī, Abū l-Qāsim ar-Rāghib. *Al-Mufradāt fī Gharīb al-Qur'ān*. Edited by Muḥammad Sa'īd. Tehran, n.d.

Izutsu, Toshihiko. *Ethico-Religious Concepts in the Qur'ān*. Montreal, 1966.

Al-Jazarī, Shams ad-Dīn. *Ghāya an-Nihāya fī Tabaqāt al-Qurrā'*. Edited by Gotthelf Bergstrasser. Cairo, 1933.

Jomier, Jacques. "Le nom divin 'al-Raḥmān' dans le Coran." *Mélanges Louis Massignon*, Damascus, 1957, II, 361-81.

Al-Jurjānī, Abū l-Ḥasan al-Ḥusayn. *At-Ta'rīfāt*. Edited by G. Flügel. Leipzig, 1845.

Lane, E.W. *An Arabic-English Lexicon*. Edited by Stanley Lane-Poole. 8 vols. London, 1863-93.

Macdonald, D.B. *Development of Religious Attitude and Life in Islam*. Beyrut, 1965.

—. and Masse, H. *et al.* "Djinn". *Encyclopaedia of Islam* (new ed.), III, 546-50.

Al-Makkī, Abū Ṭālib. *Qūt al-Qulūb*. 2 vols. Egypt, 1961/1381.

Al-Marāghī, Aḥmad Muṣṭafā. *Tafsīr al-Marāghī*. 10 vols. 2nd ed. Egypt, 1373/1953 — 1380/1961.

Al-Munāwī, 'Abd ar-Ra'ūf. *Al-Kawākib ad-Durriyya*. Edited by Maḥmūd Ḥasan Rabī'. 2 vols. Cairo, 1938/1357.

Al-Muzanī, Abū Ibrāhīm Ismā'īl Ibn Yaḥyā. *Al-Mukhtaṣar aṣ-Ṣaghīr*. Bulaq, 1321-26 A.H.

Nakamura, Kojiro. *Ghazali on Prayer*. Tokyo, Japan, 1973.

An-Nasā'ī Abū 'Abd ar-Raḥmān Ibn Shu'ayb. *Sunan*.8 vols. Egypt, 1383/1964.

An-Nawawī. *Tahdhīb al-Asmā' wa l-Lughāt*. 4 vols. Egypt, n.d.

Penrice, John. *A Dictionary and Glossary of the Kor-ān*. London, 1873.

Quasem, M.A. *The Ethics of al-Ghazālī:a Composite Ethics in Islam*. Foreword by W. Montgomery Watt. Revised Ph.D. thesis.

2nd ed. New York, 1978.

—. "Al-Ghazālī's Conception of Happiness." *Arabica,* XXII, 153-61.

—. *The Jewels of the Qur'ān:al-Ghazālī's Theory*. Malaysia, 1977.

Al-Qushayrī, Abū l-Qāsim. *Laṭā'if al-Ishārāt*. Edited by Ibrāhīm. 5 vols. Cairo, n.d.

Rahbar, Daud. *God of Justice: a study in the ethical doctrine of the Qur'ān*. Leiden, 1960.

—. "Reflections on the Tradition of Qur'ānic Exegesis." *Muslim World,* LII (1962), 269-307.

Ringgren, Helmer, "The Conception of Faith in the Qur'ān." *Oriens,* IV (1951), 1-20.

Roberts, Robert. *The Social Laws of the Qorān*. 2nd ed. London, 1971.

Aṣ-Ṣāliḥ, Ṣubḥī. *Mabāḥith fī 'Ulūm al-Qur'ān*. 5th ed. Beirut, 1968.

As-Sarrāj, Abū Naṣr. *Kitāb al-Luma'*. Edited by R.A. Nicholson, London, 1963.

Shahid, Irfan. "A Contribution to Koranic Exegesis." *Arabic and Islamic Studies in honour of Hamilton A.R. Gibb.* Leiden, 1965, pp. 563-80.

Al-Shamma, S.H. *The Ethical System underlying the Qur'ān.* Tübingen, 1959.

Ash-Shurunbalālī, Ibn 'Ammār. *Matn Nūr al-Īḍāḥ*. Cairo, 1389/1969.

Streck, M. "Ḳāf". *Encyclopaedia of Islam,* II, 614f.

As-Sulamī. *Ṭabaqāt aṣ-Ṣūfiyya al-Kubrā*. Edited by Nūr ad-Dīn. Egypt, 1953/1372.

As-Suyūṭī, Jalāl ad-Dīn. *Al-Itqān fī 'Ulūm al-Qur'ān*. 3rd ed. Cairo, 1370/1951.

—. *Lubāb an-Nuqūl fī Asbāb an-Nuzūl*. 2nd ed. Egypt, n.d.

—. and al-Maḥalli, Jalāl ad-Dīn. *Tafsīr al-Jalālayn*. On the margins of al-Qur'an al-Karīm (bi-r-rasm al-'Uthmānī). Beirut, n.d.

Aṭ-Ṭabarī, Muḥammad Ibn Jarīr, *Jāmi' al-Bayān 'an Ta'wīl Āi al-Qur'ān*. 12 vols. 2nd ed. Egypt, 1373/1954.

—. *Tārīkh al-Umam wa l-Mulūk*. Egypt, n.d.

At-Tahānawī, Muḥammad A'lā Ibn 'Alī. *Kashf Isṭilāḥāt al-Funūn*. Bayrut, 1966.

At-Tirmidhī, Abū 'Īsā Muḥammad. *Sunan*. 13 vols. Egypt,

1931-34.
Walī Allāh, Shāh. *Al-Fawz al-Kabīr fī Uṣūl at-Tafsīr*. Karachi, Pakistan, n.d.
Watt, W. Montgomery. *Companion to the Qur'ān*. London, 1967.
—. *The Formative Period of Islamic Thought*. Edinburgh, 1973.
—. "Ahl al-Ṣuffa". *Encyclopaedia of Islam* (new ed.), I, 266f.
—. " 'Ā'isha bint Abī Bakr". *Encyclopaedia of Islam* (new ed.), I, 307f.
Az-Zabīdī, Sayyid Murtaḍā. *Itḥāf as-Sāda al-Muttaqīn bi-Sharḥ Asrār Iḥyā' 'Ulūm ad-Dīn*. 10 vols. Egypt, 1311 A.H.
Az-Zajāj. *I'rāb al-Qur'ān*. 3 vols. Edited by Ibrāhīm al-Abyārī. Cairo, 1384/1965.
Az-Zamakhsharī, Abū l-Qāsim Jār Allāh. *Al-Kashshāf 'an Ḥaqā'iq at-Tanzīl*. 4 vols. Egypt, 1385/1966.
Az-Zanjānī, Abū 'Abd Allāh. *Tārīkh al-Qur'ān*. 3rd ed. Beirut, 1388/1969.

Al-Qur'ān al-Karīm (bi-r-rasm al-'Uthmānī). Edited in Egypt, n.d.

INDEX

(The Arabic article *al-*, with its variants such as *an, ash, ad, at, as,* is disregarded in the alphabetical arrangement. The articles 'the', 'a' and 'an' before English language titles are also not taken into consideration.)

GENERAL INDEX

GENERAL INDEX

INDEX OF QUR'ANIC SURAS AND VERSES CITED

a) Index of Qur'anic Suras Cited

b) Index of Qur'anic Verses Cited

INDEX OF QUR'ANIC SURAS AND VERSES CITED

(The numberings of suras and verses are
as in the Egyptian edition of the Qur'an)